CARDS FOR KIDS

CARDS FOR KIDS
Games, Tricks & Amazing Facts

by Elin McCoy

drawings by Tom Huffman

MACMILLAN PUBLISHING COMPANY
New York

Maxwell Macmillan Canada
Toronto

Maxwell Macmillan International
New York   Oxford   Singapore   Sydney

FOR GAVIN

Macmillan Publishing Company
866 Third Avenue
New York, NY   10022

Maxwell Macmillan Canada, Inc.
1200 Eglinton Avenue East
Suite 200
Don Mills, Ontario M3C 3N1

Macmillan Publishing Company is part of the Maxwell Communication
Group of Companies.

First edition
Printed in the United States of America
10 9 8 7 6 5 4 3 2 1
The text of this book is set in 12 pt. ITC Cheltenham Light.
The illustrations are rendered in pen and ink.

Library of Congress Cataloging-in-Publication Data

McCoy, Elin.
Cards for kids / by Elin McCoy ; illustrations by Tom Huffman. — 1st ed.
p.   cm.
Includes index.
Summary: Introduces a variety of card games, card tricks, and card trivia.
ISBN 0-02-765461-3
1. Card games—Juvenile literature. [1. Card games.   2. Card tricks.] I. Huffman,
Tom, ill. II. Title
GV1244.M37 1991   795.4—dc20   91-11373

ACKNOWLEDGMENTS

My first thanks go to my family—my husband, John F. Walker, and my son, Gavin McCoy Walker—for reading the manuscript, making suggestions, trying out games and tricks, and providing love and encouragement. My sister, Sharon McCoy, helped out by researching books on cards in the Cornell University Library.

A very special thanks to the Washington Montessori School in New Preston, Connecticut, where I held after-school card game workshops, and to all the kids in the workshops who tried out the games and tricks in this book and helped invent some: Jackson Barry, Zachary Bernard, Jonathan Brody-Felber, Emily Broidrick, Eliza Fitzgerald, Fiona Hopper, Jeffrey Jock, Galen Largay, Bryan Leifert, Benjamin Maitland-Lewis, Brett Markman, Ashley Merz, Katherine Rahilly, Justin Scott, Adrian Stier, Andrea Stier, Benjamin Tomek, Michael Walter, and Rebecca Walter. Additional thanks to Cherry Thurlow for arranging the workshops, to Jackson Barry for his free-form card tower design and invented game, and to Zachary, Fiona, Ashley, Galen, and Rebecca for their imaginative game ideas.

I'd also like to thank my friend, Roberta Satow Wool, and her two sons, Jason and Matthew, for reading the book, trying some games, and commenting on them. A big thanks to Rebecca Elin Blomquist, my cousin, who provided ideas and help, and to Tyler Norman, another cousin, who shared his expertise on card tricks.

I am deeply indebted to Margery B. Griffith, the director of The Playing Card Museum at the United States Playing Card Company in Cincinnati, Ohio, who shared her vast knowledge of cards, answered many questions, provided copies of articles and bibliographic information, and names of people and organizations to contact. I am also grateful for the information on the history of playing cards compiled by Ron Decker, curator of the museum.

Thanks are also due Mr. Gene Hochman of Boynton Beach, Florida, an antique card dealer, for answering my questions. The office of British Information Services provided helpful information on British taxes levied on playing cards.

The New York Public Library, as always, provided help, as did the library of the New-York Historical Society. I'm also thankful to Deborah Custer, librarian of the Kent Memorial Library in Kent, Connecticut, for obtaining a number of needed books and for patience in awaiting their return.

Last, I'd like to thank my editor, Susan Wilkes, for her help and careful editing.

CONTENTS

INTRODUCTION

When I was about five years old, I learned to play cards at my family's summer cottage in Michigan. My cousins and I whiled away hours on rainy days playing Go Fish, War, Concentration, Poker, and lots of other card games. We usually played in the boathouse among fishing gear, sails, oars, paddles, and who knows what else. My mom loved solitaire games so we learned those, too. Now my son is doing the same thing with his cousins! That's why I wrote this book.

The nice thing about cards is that there are so many different things you can do with them, even in a small space like an airplane seat or car. You can play simple or complicated card games, ones that take a long time to play or only ten minutes, and games for just one person or a whole group. You can make up your own card games and change the rules when you feel like it. You can spend hours building a house from cards or entertain your friends with foolproof card tricks.

This book will tell you everything you need to know to have fun with cards. Here's how to use it. The first part of the book is all about the things you need to know before you play—how to count cards, what a suit is, how to shuffle, cut, deal, and score. If you already know how to play some card games, skip most of this part. But be sure to take a look at Card Manners (page 23) just to remind yourself how to be a good sport. And if you are trying to teach some games to a preschooler, read the note on how to play with them. When you have time, take a look at the amazing facts about cards, stories of famous cardplayers, and secrets of cardsharps and card cheats. There is a card glossary at the end of the book on page 146. There are lots of special terms in card playing, so if you see a term you don't understand, here's where to look it up.

The second part of the book will tell you how to play different card games that are popular with kids. They're arranged from easiest to hardest, followed by poker and solitaire games. The section on poker games will also tell you about poker chips, strategy, and how to keep a poker face.

The third part will tell you how to make your own card games and give you some examples.

Finally, the fourth part contains some foolproof card tricks and stunts for you to try.

If you are looking for a particular game or trick, just look in the index, of course!

Hope you have fun. That's what playing with cards is all about.

I

A Guide
to the Cards

COUNTING CARDS

The first thing you need to know is that a deck of cards is a set of cards, usually fifty-two, that have numbers and pictures on them.

The number cards, which are also called *spot* cards, have a number in two corners and *spots* or *pips* in the center. These will either be hearts, diamond shapes, cloverlike shapes called *clubs,* or little spearhead shapes called *spades.* The number of spots on the card matches the numeral on it, like this:

The number cards are: ace, which usually counts as one, 2, 3, 4, 5, 6, 7, 8, 9, and 10.

When you are counting points, which you do in some games, remember that number cards have the same value as the number on them. A 3 is worth 3 points. A 10 is worth 10 points. That's called the *face value.*

The odd card in all this is the ace. In some games an ace is worth 1 point, but often it's worth 11 points. Sometimes it can be both.

How did the ace get its name? The word comes from the Latin word *as* (pronounced ace), which means a unit or one.

Cards are also called *high* or *low*. A 3 is a low card, 5 is higher, and a 10 is usually the highest of the number cards. The ace can be the lowest (when it equals 1) or the highest (when it equals 11). Game directions always tell you whether the ace is high or low.

CARD ROYALTY

The picture cards, which are also called *face* cards or *court* cards, have pictures of royalty on them. The Jack has the letter *J* in two corners, the Queen has a *Q* in two corners, and the King has a *K* in two corners, like this:

All these cards are worth more than a number card, but they don't have any special number value. The Jack is the lowest face card, then comes the Queen, and the King is the highest. But in games where the ace is high, it is higher than the King.

4

Court or royalty cards, showing Kings and Queens, were in the earliest decks of cards in Europe; the American kind of card deck came from Europe.

Have you noticed the crazy clothes the King, Queen, and Jack wear? These costumes are based on what real kings and queens in England wore during the 1500s.

There haven't been many changes in court cards since then.

THE STORY OF THE JOKER

There are lots of other strange things about the cards we use. One of the strangest is the two extra cards that come with every deck, the jokers. Sometimes the joker is pictured as a jester dressed in colorful medieval clothes complete with cap and bells, like this one:

But sometimes jokers have other pictures or designs, like horses.

Even though card decks always come with jokers, most card games don't use them. They are only used in card games as wild cards. (A wild card can be whatever number or suit a player wishes.)

Jokers are also useful if you lose one card in a deck —you can just write that number on the joker card.

How did the joker get into card decks? It's an American invention. It became part of the regular deck during the 1860s in the United States because of a game called *euchre*. This popular game needed a deck with an extra card that was higher than all the others, so manufacturers put a blank card called the *euchre* card in each deck. Supposedly, the word *euchre* was misspelled by people and eventually became the word Joker.

THE TRUTH ABOUT
ONE-EYED JACKS

If you look at the four Jacks in a deck of cards, you'll notice that two of them are in profile, with only one eye showing. These are called the one-eyed Jacks. In poker games, players sometimes make

these Jacks wild cards. Lots of people think these one-eyed Jacks must have had some special meaning in the past, but they didn't. In early card decks Kings, Queens, Jacks, and other figures were shown many different ways: standing, on horseback, with a full face showing, in profile, and so on. It just happened that the early card decks made in Rouen, France, had one-eyed Jacks in their decks. These were the decks that most printers in England copied, and the English deck is the one that came to America.

WHAT'S A SUIT?

Card decks are divided into four suits of thirteen cards each. Look at the cards in your deck. Do you see a special design on the face of each one? Those are the symbols for the four suits. They are sometimes called *spots* or *pips*. Two suits are red: hearts ♥ and diamonds ♦. Two suits are black: clubs ♣ and spades ♠. The thirteen cards in each suit go from ace to King or two to ace.

Suits have been part of card playing for centuries. One set of early Korean cards had seven suits. Early Islamic decks used four suits, the way we do, but the Islamic suits were coins, cups, swords, and polo sticks. Some experts think they represented people serving the

sultan. The oldest European decks used four suits, too, which stood for the four parts of medieval life. Cups represented the church, coins, the merchants, swords, the nobles and soldiers, and batons, the peasants and farmers. (These symbols are still used on cards in Spain and Italy.) In Germany hearts, acorns, leaves, and bells were used. Around 500 years ago, card makers in France invented the suit signs we use today.

AMAZING FACTS ABOUT CARDS & FAMOUS CARDPLAYERS

No one knows who invented the first card games. Historians and card experts think cards were invented in China over 1,000 years ago.

Playing cards first came from Europe to the Americas with sailors on Columbus's voyage in 1492.

There weren't any numbers on cards in the first European decks. Players had to count the number of suit symbols on each one.

Cards have been made in all shapes and sizes—square, oblong, even round.

Early cards in America were made from leaves and from the skin of sheep and deer. Some card decks at the beginning of this century were even made from aluminum.

The earliest cards in Europe were very, very expensive because each deck had to be made and painted by hand. Ordinary people couldn't even afford to buy cards until the printing press was invented in the 1400s. Printing cards was as important to printers as printing books.

♦

Playing card companies have secret recipes for the paper and coatings used in making cards. The paper is laminated and coated with china clay, titanium dioxide, castor oil, and other ingredients so you can't see through it; then it's run through a crusher, which smooths it before the cards are printed, varnished, and cut apart.

Card playing was illegal in the Puritan colonies of seventeenth-century New England. Adults paid a fine if they were caught once. The second time they could be whipped in public—even if they just had a pack of cards in their house.

♠

George Washington loved to play cards. He recorded in his diary just how much he won and lost at cards each week.

♥

Thomas Jefferson played cards to relax while he was writing the Declaration of Independence.

♦

Benjamin Franklin printed and sold cards and used them in some of his electrical experiments.

♣

Playing cards were once taxed everywhere. That's how the strange design on the ace of spades started in England in 1628. So people couldn't avoid paying a tax on each deck of cards, the government passed a law requiring card printers to have a special design for the

ace of spades and to purchase a tax stamp to put on the design before the deck could be sold. The tax lasted for almost 350 years.

♠

Wild Bill Hickok was shot in the back during a poker game in the Nuttal and Mann Saloon in Deadwood, South Dakota, in 1876. Even today poker players call the card combination Hickok was holding— a pair of aces and a pair of 8s—a "Dead Man's Hand."

♥

Women were hot card players in western boom towns. One, Doña Gertrudes de Barcelo of Santa Fe, won enough money at Three Card Monte (see page 40) to buy supplies for the American Army during the 1848 Mexican War.

♦

Annie Oakley, the best sharpshooter in the West, used the ace of hearts in one of her most important tricks. She pinned it on a tree twenty-five yards away, then fired twenty-five shots in twenty-seven seconds to shoot away the heart in the center.

♣

During the Civil War, card decks were changed to be more patriotic. Some had Union generals instead of Kings; others had American flags and stars for the red suits and the shield and American eagles for the black ones; still another had infantry officers for Kings, god-desses of liberty for Queens, and artillery officers for Jacks.

♠

The biggest poker game in American gambling history was probably the one that took place in 1900 at the Waldorf-Astoria Hotel in New York City. The people playing were a famous poker player named Bet-a-Million Gates and some of his friends. That game involved a million dollars.

♥

The longest card game ever played is probably a bridge game played by four students at Edinburgh University in Scotland in 1972. It lasted 180 hours! That's according to the Guinness Book of World Records.

♦

The most popular card games in America today are Bridge, Poker, and Gin Rummy.

♣

More than 100 million decks of cards are sold in the United States every year.

♠

The most money ever paid for a deck of cards was over $100,000. The Metropolitan Museum of Art in New York City paid that in 1983 for a deck of Flemish cards made in the fifteenth century.

SECRETS OF CARDSHARPS AND CARD CHEATS

The history of card playing is part of the history of gambling. Playing cards for money is as old as card games are. People who want to win money at cards and don't care what they have to do to win sometimes cheat. In all centuries, in all countries (even today), there have been professional and amateur card cheats called *cardsharps* who try to win by using all sorts of ingenious methods.

During the sixteenth, seventeenth, and eighteenth centuries in Paris, France, card sharping was everywhere. At the end of the 1700s the city had 4,000 places to gamble. Some people lost everything they owned to cardsharps. One way they cheated was to rub the backs of important cards with a pumice stone, which left a slightly rough spot on the card. The cardsharp would know what the card was just by touching the back. Some cardsharps used extreme methods. One story tells about a famous cardsharp from Paris named Signor Calzado, who visited Cuba in the 1860s. Supposedly, he sent a huge supply of marked cards to Havana by ship. As soon as he arrived, he bought every pack of cards in town and then waited for the boat with the marked cards to dock. Guess who won most of the cards games while he was there?

In the United States, the boats that traveled on the Mississippi River from 1840 to 1870 usually had one or more professional cardsharps on board. They were noted for winning lots of money from

unsuspecting passengers. Often they worked in pairs, using cigar smoke rings to signal to each other: one smoke ring meant one pair, two rings, two pairs, three meant three of a kind. Some cardsharps gave signals by twirling their cane in a special way. The card game they used to trick people most often was Three Card Monte (see page 40 to learn how to play it).

Cardsharps were such a problem on the trains during the nineteenth century that conductors were told to make all people playing Three Card Monte get off.

In the Wild West most cheating was done during poker games. If someone was caught cheating, that was considered enough reason to shoot him! A jury would consider it self-defense.

Here are some of the clever methods cardsharps have used to cheat at cards. One kind of cheating is knowing who has what cards. That helps a cardsharp know when he won't get the cards he needs, whether someone else has a better hand, and how to bet.

Peeking

If a card cheat is dealing, he can squeeze the front two edges of the top card between his middle finger and thumb to glimpse at the number or letter in the corner of the card before he deals it. That's called *a bubble peek*. He can also peek at the bottom card of the deck as he is squaring it after shuffling and cutting. A cheat may drop a card deliberately and peek at his neighbor's hand as he leans over to pick it up. He may peek when he draws a card from the stock by lifting up the two top cards at the inner edge. He can glance at the corner of the second card, then let it drop down on the stock as he picks up the top card. Then he knows which card his opponent will draw. This is especially useful in Gin Rummy. Some card cheats even hide a mirror under the table near the dealer so they can see the underside of the cards he's dealing. (Make sure that you're not sitting with your back to a mirror when you're playing! The other players will be able to see your cards easily.)

Marked Cards

Card cheats sometimes mark the backs of the cards in some way so they know what a card is just by glancing at the back of it. One kind of marked deck has a different spot in the back design blocked out on each card. The patterns are codes that tell the cheater the number (and sometimes the suit, too) of that particular card. If you flip through the cards quickly, it's easy to detect this kind of marked deck. If the cards are marked, the dots will look as though they are jumping around.

Cardsharps also mark cards by roughing the edges of special cards with sandpaper. Or they trim the sides of high cards so they are very slightly narrower than the low ones. That's called *belly stripping*.

All these things have to be done *before* a game. But cheats can mark cards while they play, too. A cheat may *nail* special cards by digging his thumbnail into the side edge of a card, making a little

15

nick. Where he makes the nick tells him what the card is the next time he sees it. Pegging is another method. The cheat has a Band-Aid on his thumb or finger with a sharpened thumbtack in it, like this:

He pricks the face of Kings and aces with it, which makes a small bump in the card's back.

A Stacked Deck

Another kind of cheating is arranging the cards so you get the ones you want. A sneaky dealer has the best chance to cheat this way.

Before the game, a card cheat can arrange the cards in a deck carefully so that when he deals he will get the hand he wants. If five people are going to play, he may make the fifth and tenth cards aces, for example, so he'll get a pair of aces. Then, during the game, he switches this arranged deck—called a *stacked deck*—with the one the players have been using.

To switch decks, a cardsharp waits until he is the dealer. Then he may spread a handkerchief on his lap, slide the stacked deck from a pocket into his left hand and pull the just-cut deck to the edge of the table in his right hand. He can let the just-cut deck fall into his lap and wrap it in his handkerchief, as he sneaks the stacked deck onto the table. So people won't notice what he is doing, a cheat will sneeze or spill his drink while he is switching decks.

Holding Out

Sometimes cardsharps hide one or more cards—usually aces or high cards—and slip them out into their hand when they need them.

Often they hide them in a sleeve. That's where the expression, "He's got an ace up his sleeve," came from. There is even a special sleeve machine that cheats may strap on their arms under their sleeves. They can easily slide a card up into the machine and pull it out later without anyone noticing. But they can also just hide a card under a knee or in an armpit.

Sooner or later, though, people catch on to a cardsharp. That's why they have never stayed long in one place.

Most cheating that kids do involves peeking at someone's hand. If one of your friends keeps peeking, have everyone sit farther apart so he or she can't peek without looking really obvious. And if kids really want to cheat, play the game I Doubt It (page 64). That's a game where cheating is necessary.

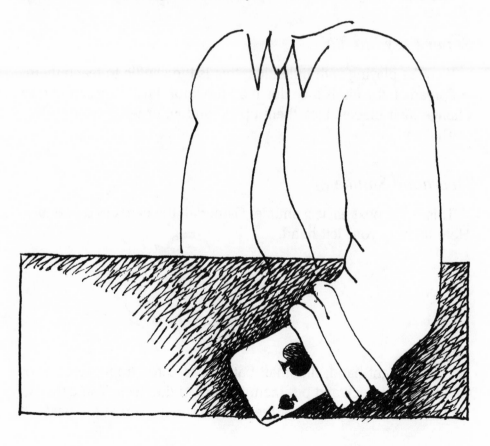

HOW TO SHUFFLE AND WHY

Before you start a game, you want the cards to be completely mixed so that suits and numbers aren't in any special order. (Otherwise one person might get all the high cards or a lot of pairs, and that wouldn't be fair.) Mixing the deck is called *shuffling.* You should shuffle the cards twice before each game.

There are easy and hard ways to shuffle. Start with the easiest.

Super Easy Shuffle

If you're playing with little kids, this is the shuffle to teach them.

Spread all the cards face down on the floor. Push them around to change their places. Pick them up in random order.

That's it!

Overhand Shuffle

This is the next easiest shuffle. Gather all the cards into one pile. Hold them in your left hand.

With your right hand, lift small batches of cards from the back or middle of the deck and put them in front of the deck. You can also lift batches from the front of the deck and put them at the back.

The Riffle Shuffle

Kids younger than six have difficulty with this shuffle, mostly because their hands are too small. When you're learning how to do it, look carefully at the pictures below. Usually it's easier to understand how to do this shuffle from pictures than to read about it.

Gather the cards into one pile, then divide it into two piles that are about equal. Place them so the short ends are next to one another, like this:

Hold one pile in each hand. Your thumb should be at one end, your little, ring, and middle fingers at the other, and your index finger curled to rest on top of the pile, like this:

Bend the cards up at one end with your thumbs. Let go of one card from one pile, then one from the other pile by lifting up your thumbs. The cards should drop gently so they overlap one another. Keep letting go of one card at a time until they all overlap, like this:

19

Slide them together into a single pile, like this:

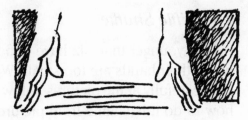

Then hold the deck and tap one long side against the table to straighten the cards.

Don't be discouraged if it takes you a while to learn how to shuffle this way.

Just keep practicing!

HOW TO CUT CARDS AND WHY

Cutting the cards after they're shuffled helps prevent cheating. It's an extra way to mix the cards in case the players have seen the bottom card while the deck is being shuffled, or if the dealer arranged them in a special way so a particular player would get the good cards. You don't *have* to cut the cards. But most people do.

After the dealer shuffles the deck twice, he straightens and squares it face down on the table. The player to his left is the one who cuts the deck. The player lifts up the top part of the deck, puts it down on the table, and then puts the bottom part on top of it.

That's all there is to it!

HOW TO DEAL AND
WHO GOES FIRST

Before you can play a game, you have to hand out cards. That's called *dealing*. The dealer is the person you choose to hand out the cards. Usually the dealer is the person who shuffles the cards, too.

Choosing a Dealer

There are lots of fair ways to choose a dealer. Here are two: (1) Spread the cards face down on the table and have every player pick a card. Whoever has the highest card is the dealer. Say in advance whether ace is high or low. (2) Take turns drawing cards from a face-down deck until someone draws an ace. Then that person is the first dealer.

Usually a person is only a dealer for one game. Then the player on his left becomes the next dealer. Sometimes the person who wins the game is the next dealer.

How to Deal

Hold the deck of cards face down, keeping your hand across the bottom card. (You don't want anyone to see it.) Give the top card to the player on your left. Give the next card to the player on her left. Keep dealing to the left around the table, ending with the dealer. Then start a new round. Always deal one card at a time unless the game directions say to deal more. Try not to let players see the faces of the cards as you deal.

Who Goes First

The player to the left of the dealer is almost always the first one to play her cards.

KEEPING SCORE

There are two ways to keep score when you're playing cards. For both you need pencil and paper.

One way is just to keep track of who wins each game. Write the names of the players at the top of the paper. Each time someone wins, make a short vertical line below their name, like this:

Brett	Justin	Jeff
III	IIII	₩₩Ⱶ I

When someone has won a fifth time, make the fifth line a diagonal one across the others as shown above. When that player wins again, start a new group of five marks. This way of scoring makes it easy to add up the number of games each person has won. You just count by fives and add on any extra marks. Here's what Jeff's score was at the end of the game:

₩₩Ⱶ ₩₩Ⱶ ₩₩Ⱶ II

Did you get seventeen?

You can use this method of scoring for any games in which you count the number of cards, pairs, sets, or tricks to determine the winner. That means games like: Slapjack, War, Old Maid, Stealing Bundles, Go Fish, Authors, Concentration, and others.

If you start playing a different game, start a new score sheet, too.

The other way to keep score is to add up points, which you use for games like: Casino, Gin Rummy, or Hearts. In these card games, you get points for having special cards, and some figuring is necessary to decide who won.

Here's the way Ben and Bryan scored their Casino game:

	Ben	Bryan	
most cards	3	2	big Casino
most spades	1	1	little Casino
ace	1	1	ace
ace	1	1	ace
	6	5	

There is a third way to keep score—by using chips or counters the way you do in Poker. When the game is over, the winner is the one with the most chips.

But remember that you don't *have* to keep score. Sometimes that just makes who won and who lost too big a deal.

CARD MANNERS

Card manners don't have anything to do with the actual rules of a game. They are concerned with the way players usually handle the cards, treat one another, and what they do about mistakes. This list will give you some ideas, but find out how *your* friends want to play. Some kids like to collect the cards and deal all over again no matter what the mistake.

1. Agree on the rules of the game ahead of time. For example, how you'll score; what you have to do to win;

LETS FOLLOW THE RULES!

and what you'll do about mistakes. Then play by the rules.

2. Deal all cards face down (unless the rules for a game say to deal them face up). If a card lands face up by mistake, bury it in the deck so no one knows where it is. Deal a new card to that player.

3. Wait until everyone gets their cards before you touch or pick up yours.

4. Don't peek at anyone's cards.

5. Hold your cards so that no one can see them. Don't hold them far out or down so that other players can't help seeing them.

6. Wait your turn to play during the game.

7. Here's how to act when you win: Don't brag about it. That just makes everyone feel jealous.

8. Here's how to act when you lose: Don't argue. A good loser is someone who is cheerful and generous to those who win. It's good sportsmanship to congratulate another player—"You sure had a great hand," or "You sure were lucky. Maybe I'll win next time." Remember that a card game is just a game. If you're losing a lot, suggest playing a different game.

9. Be a good sport. That means playing the best you can—without cheating—and not getting mad when you lose. It means recognizing that no one can win all the time.

PLAYING CARDS WITH PRESCHOOLERS

Little kids aged three to five love to play cards, but to make it fun for them you have to make games easy for them to follow and understand.

First of all, their hands are too small to do a regular shuffle or fan their cards. But they can learn the Super Easy Shuffle (page 18). And instead of holding cards in their hands, they can lean the cards against piles of books or a pillow.

That way they can sort them and see them easily.

Next, don't play with the whole deck. That many cards is usually too confusing. Besides, little kids may not know all the numbers and letters and they may have trouble telling the picture cards apart. So start with aces, 2s, 3s, 4s, 5s, and 6s. Use only one set of picture cards—Jacks are best. Then add more cards as kids are able to recognize them. Try to find a deck that has large numerals, too. There are new ones designed for older people who have eye problems. These are great for little kids!

Choosing a Game

Pick games that have simple rules. Games in this book that are fun for preschoolers are: In the Hat, Pig, Slapjack (with Jacks as the only picture cards), Concentration (use only twenty cards), Easy Go Fish, and Snip, Snap, Snorem.

Play a new game at least five times with the cards face up, first.

Sometimes you'll have to change the rules if a game turns out to be too hard.

Winning and Losing

Little kids find it harder to lose than older kids do. So play together in a more cooperative way. For example, you can help each other remember where a card was in the game Concentration, and check one another's hands for pairs in Easy Go Fish.

You can also change the way you talk about winning. Instead of shouting, "I won and you lost! Ha! Ha!" you can say, "Hooray! Look at all the pairs we both made!" or "Great! We've used up all the cards!" or "You got the ace, so you deal next." When you focus on who won and who lost, little kids end up trying to cheat, change the rules, argue, feel angry and upset, or just don't want to play anymore.

2
Forty-Two Fun Games from Pig to Poker

These are arranged from easiest to hardest.

Number
of
Players
2 to 4

IN THE HAT

Even a two- or three-year-old can learn to play this very simple card game. All you do is toss cards into a hat a few feet away.

Dealing

You don't have to deal in this game. Just make sure that each player has the same number of cards. Use only ten cards each for very little kids, but older ones can each use a deck of fifty-two cards. You'll also need a hat with a shape such as a cowboy hat or straw beach hat.

> **Hint 1:** Use a metal pot, large plastic bowl or small box if you don't have a hat.

How to Play

Put the hat on the floor with the open side up. Make a line two or three feet away with chalk or masking tape. (Change the distance if this turns out to be too easy or too hard.) Take turns trying to toss cards into the hat. Keep tossing until you miss. Then it's the next player's turn.

The one who gets rid of all their cards first is the winner.

> **Hint 2:** Hold the corner of the card between your thumb and first finger, like this:
>
>
> Your thumb should be on top of the card when you throw.

PIG

This very silly game is more fun when a whole bunch of kids play. The most important thing is to keep your eyes on the other players so you won't end up being the Pig.

Dealing

From a regular deck (fifty-two cards) remove one set of four of the same number or picture for each player. It doesn't matter which sets you take out. If you have five players, you need twenty cards—four each. (How many will you have for ten players?) With thirteen kids you'll use the whole deck.

Shuffle the sets of cards together and cut. Then deal four cards to each player, one at a time.

How to Play

Arrange the cards in your hand so that matching cards are together. When the dealer says, "Go," all players quickly pick one card they don't want and put it face down to their left.

> **Strategy hint:** You're trying to get four cards that match. So if you have a pair, put down one of your other cards.

Then everyone picks up the face-down card to their right. If it matches a card in their hand they put it next to that card.

As soon as the dealer says, "Go," again, everyone chooses another card to pass to the left. Players keep passing and picking up cards trying to be the first to get four matching cards.

When you get four of a kind, you stop passing cards and put a finger on your nose. Everyone else must stop passing, too, and quickly put their fingers on their noses. The last one to do so is the PIG. Whoever loses five times is the prize PIG and has to shout, "Oink! Oink!"

P.S. In this game, it's okay to tell the player next to you to hurry up and pass.

SLAPJACK

This is another easy, fast, fun game. When some of the players are little kids, it can get really noisy and wild. You want to be the first to slap each card with a Jack on it so you'll end up with all the cards.

Dealing

Shuffle and cut the cards. Deal out all the cards, one at a time. It's okay if some players get an extra card.

Players make a neat face-down pile of their cards without looking at them. Don't cheat!

P.S. With three- and four-year-olds, take out all the face cards except the Jacks before dealing. This makes spotting the Jacks much easier.

How to Play

Are you the player on the dealer's left? You start the game by quickly turning up the top card in your pile and placing it face up in the center of the table. Turn it up away from you so that everyone, including you, sees the card at the same time. Otherwise it's not fair.

32

Then the person on your left turns up a card as fast as possible and so on around the table. It's more exciting when you go as quickly as you can. When a Jack is turned up everyone tries to be the first to slap their hand down on it and keep it there. The player who slaps first (theirs is the hand on the bottom) wins all the cards in the center pile and puts them at the bottom of their own pile. The player on the winner's left throws out a new card to start the next round.

If by mistake you slap a card that isn't a Jack, you have to give a card from your pile to each player.

If you lose all your cards, you can get back into the game by being the first to slap the next Jack.

The player to get all fifty-two cards wins. But if that takes too long, you can end the game when the first player is out. The one with the most cards is the winner.

P.S. 1. You have to turn up the card and slap it with the *same* hand.

P.S. 2. Don't slap too hard! Someone's hand may be underneath.

CONCENTRATION

Don't start playing this game unless you can really pay attention to what's going on! The person with the best memory will be the winner. And guess what? Often the youngest player wins. The point is to use your memory to help you collect the most pairs.

Number
of
Players
2 to 6

Best with 2

Dealing

Shuffle and cut the cards. Spread all the cards face down on a table so they don't overlap. You can arrange them in face-down rows instead.

Hint 1: The game is easier when you arrange the cards in rows.
Hint 2: When playing with younger children (under six), use only twenty-six cards (half a deck), making sure there is one pair of each rank (Kings, 2s, 6s, etc.).

How to Play

The dealer starts. He turns any two cards face up, one at a time. If they make a pair (like two 10s or two aces), he puts them face down in front of himself and then turns over two more cards. A player keeps his turn as long as he turns over pairs. If the cards don't match, he turns them face down again exactly where he found them. Now it's the next player's turn.

You can guess the strategy to win. If you pay close attention to the cards that are turned back down again, you'll be able to remember where a lot of different cards are. Then when you turn up a King, you'll remember where its match is.

When all the cards have been picked up, the player with the most cards wins.

EASY GO FISH

Here's a very easy version of Go Fish, one that's fun even for four-year-olds. All you have to do to win is collect the most pairs—two 6s or two Queens, for example.

Dealing

Shuffle and cut the cards. Deal five cards, one at a time, to each player. Spread the rest of the deck face down in the center of the table.

How to Play

Before you start, see if you have any pairs in your hand. If you do, put them face up on the table.

The dealer goes first. She asks any player for a card that matches one she has. Here's an example: Adrian has one Queen, one 6, one 3, and two Jacks. He puts the two Jacks face up in front of himself. Then he says, "Rebecca, give me a Queen!" Rebecca has one, so she must hand it over. Then he asks Eliza for a 6. Eliza doesn't have one. She says, "Go fish." Adrian has to pick a card from the face-down cards in the center. If he picks a 6, he gets another turn. If he doesn't, the player on his left has the next turn and so on around the table.

Players can keep asking or fishing only as long as they get the card they asked for.

When you get a pair, you always put the cards face up in front of you.

When all the cards are gone, the player who has the most pairs wins the game.

P.S. If you run out of cards you can take one from the face-down cards.

GO FISH

Play this regular version of Go Fish with kids who are at least six years old. The object is to collect the most sets of four matching cards, like four Jacks or four 3s.

Dealing

Shuffle and cut the cards. Deal five cards, one at a time, to each player. Put the rest of the cards face down in a pile in the center of the table.

How to Play

Arrange your hand so that matching numbers or pictures are together. If you have four of a kind—that's called a *book*—put them face up in front of you.

The dealer goes first. When it's your turn, you ask any player for cards that match one you have. Suppose you have two 8s, two 6s, and one King. You say, "Katharine, do you have any 8s?" Katharine has two, so she must give you both of them. You put down the four 8s and ask Justin for 6s. He doesn't have any, and says, "Go fish." You must draw a card from the center pile. If it is a 6, you take another turn. If it isn't, the turn passes to the player on your left, and so on around the table.

Guess what! The player on your left is Katharine. She has one 6. Since she heard you ask for a 6, she knows you have at least one. When she asks you, you have to give her both your 6s. That's an example of how the game works.

Players can keep asking or fishing as long as they get the card they asked for.

When a player gets a book, he always puts them face up in a pile in front of himself.

The player who has the most books wins the game.

THREE CARD MONTE

This easy game is the same one professional gamblers used to win money from people on the Mississippi River boats during the nineteenth century. But don't you cheat!

Dealing

Take out the ace of spades, the ace of hearts, and the ace of diamonds. Give each player the same amount of poker chips.

How to Play

The dealer shows the three cards to the other players. Then she puts them face down on a table and moves them around with both hands, like this:

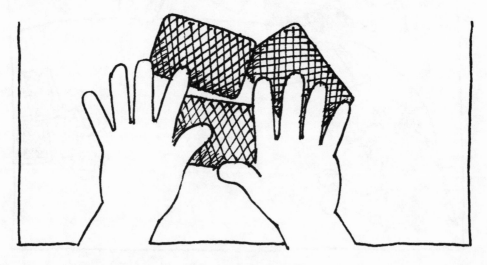

Each player watches carefully. When the dealer stops moving them, everyone tries to guess which face-down card is the ace of spades. Then each player puts a few chips on top of the card she thinks is the right guess.

When everyone has made a bet, turn the cards face up. If a player guessed right, the dealer has to pay her the same number of chips she bet. The dealer gets the chips of everyone who guessed wrong.

WAR

Number
of
Players
2 to 8

Start
with just 2

War is one of the easiest games to learn and play, but don't let that fool you! It's also very exciting, fast, and lots of fun. The whole point is to win all the cards.

Dealing

Shuffle and cut the cards. Deal one card at a time to each player until all the cards are gone. Depending on how many kids play, a few players may get an extra card. That's okay.

How to Play

Each player puts her pile of cards face down in front of herself. Then everyone turns the top card in their piles face up. Whoever has the highest card wins all the face-up cards and puts them at the bottom of her pile. (Ace is the highest in this game.) Then everyone turns over the top cards again, and so on.

So far, so good. This game gets exciting when war starts.

Here's how it happens: Two kids turn over cards that are alike. They might be two Jacks or two 10s or two 8s. The two kids have a war to see who will win all the face-up cards.

Here's what they do: Each kid takes the top card from her pile and puts it face down without looking at it. Then each player takes another card and puts it face up. Whoever has the higher face-up card wins the war, and takes all the face-up and the two face-down cards.

Keep playing until someone wins all the cards. That player is the winner.

P.S. If more than two kids are playing, the two cards that are alike have to be the highest cards played in that round to start a war. Only the two kids with matching cards are in that round of war.

SNIP, SNAP, SNOREM

In this old English game, the idea is to be the first to get rid of all your cards. Make sure you know when to say the three important words— Snip, Snap, Snorem—*before* the game starts.

Dealing

Shuffle and cut the cards. Deal two at a time to each player until all the cards are gone. If a few kids get an extra card, that's okay.

How to Play

The player on the dealer's left starts.

When it's your turn, put any one of your cards face up in the center of the table. The player to your left puts down a card with a matching number or picture if he has one and says, "Snip." But if he doesn't have one, he passes and doesn't put any card down.

The next player with a matching card says, "Snap," when putting it down, and the one with the third matching card says, "Snorem." (Now there are four cards that match in a pile.) The player who lays down the snorem card starts a new round with any card he chooses.

But suppose you have more than one matching card? You put them all down in the same turn, using the right word with each card—Snip on the first, Snap on the second, and Snorem on the third.

The winner is the first player to get rid of all his cards.

44

CHASE THE ACE

Number
of
Players
5 to 20

It's more
fun with a
big group!

Once you understand how to play this game you'll know how it got it's name. Read on!

Dealing

Shuffle and cut the cards. Deal one to each player. Put the rest of the cards, called the *stock,* to one side. You'll also need poker chips or some other counting token such as buttons. Each player starts with three.

How to Play

The player on the dealer's left begins. When it's your turn, look at your card and decide whether to keep it or trade it to the player on your left. You don't want a high card, especially not the ace, which is the highest. Your neighbor on the left *has* to trade cards if you ask.

Then your neighbor decides whether or not to trade with the player on his left, and so on around the circle. When it is the dealer's turn, he does something a little different. He or she can keep his or her card or put it face up next to the stock in a discard pile and then take the top card from the stock.

Now all players turn their cards face up. Whoever has the highest card puts one chip in the center of the table. The player to the left of the dealer deals the next round. Everyone plays until their chips are gone. The winner is the player who lasts the longest.

MENAGERIE

Be prepared for a lot of silliness when you play this game. The point is to win all the cards and you can only do this if you can make animal noises more quickly than someone else!

Dealing

Before you deal, everyone chooses an animal (cow, dog, pig, cuckoo, etc.) and makes the sound that animal would make. When everyone knows everyone else's animal call, shuffle and cut the cards. Deal one at a time to each player until all the cards are gone. If some players get an extra card that's okay.

How to Play

Stack your cards in a face-down pile in front of you. Don't peek at any of your cards.

The player on the left of the dealer starts. He turns over his top card and puts it in front of his face-down pile. Then the player on his left does the same, and so on around the circle. When someone turns up a card that matches the number or picture on the top card of another player's face-up pile, both try to be the first to make the other's animal call. Whoever gives the correct call first wins the other player's face-up card pile. The loser puts out the next card.

Here's an example of how the game works. Becky (cow) turns up a 5. Michael (cat) on her left turns up a King. Jono (horse) on his left turns up a 10. Jason (dog) on his left turns up a Queen. Then it's

Becky's turn again. She turns up a King. She quickly shouts "Meow!" before Michael makes a sound. She wins the cards in his face-up pile and puts them at the bottom of her face-down pile. Michael puts out another face-up card and everyone continues.

When you have used up all your face-down cards, you turn over your face-up pile and continue.

The player who eventually gets all the cards wins the game.

P.S. If you make the wrong call, you have to give your face-up card pile to the other player.

OLD MAID

This is an old, old game. You can use a regular deck of cards or you can use one of the special Old Maid decks sold at book, stationery, and variety stores. These contain matching pairs of characters—usually very funny ones—and one card with a picture of the "Old Maid." You could even make your own Old Maid deck.

Whichever you use, the point of the game is the same: to match all the cards in your hand, to make pairs, and not to get stuck holding the "Old Maid."

Dealing

Take out all the Queens except the Queen of clubs if you are using a regular deck of cards. That will be the "Old Maid." Then shuffle and cut the cards. Deal out all the cards, one at a time. It doesn't matter if some kids have an extra one.

How to Play

Check to see if you have any pairs. Put all your pairs face down in front of you. Then arrange the rest of your cards in a fan.

The dealer starts. When it's your turn, pull a card from the hand of the player on your left. No peeking! If you get a card that matches one in your hand, you show the pair and put it down with your other pairs. If the card doesn't make a pair, you just keep it in your hand. Don't show it to anyone. Then the player on your left turns to his left neighbor and picks a card and so on around the table.

48

When all the cards are paired, one person will be left with the Queen of clubs. That person loses the game.

> **Strategy hint:** If you have the Queen of clubs during the game, you want to get rid of it. That means someone else has to pick it out of your hand. Some kids carefully arrange their cards so the Old Maid sticks up. Usually this strategy doesn't work. A better trick is to fake out other players by having a different card stick out. Most kids will go for the *least* obvious card.

STEALING BUNDLES

Number
of
Players
2 to 4

Four is best

This is a super easy version of Casino (page 76). Expect a lot of suspense because you won't know who's going to win until the very end!

Dealing

Shuffle and cut the cards. Deal out cards one at a time until all players have four. Then put four cards from the remaining stock face up in the center of the table. When players use up the four cards in their hands, deal four more to each and so on throughout the game. When the four cards on the table are used up, deal four more from the stock.

How to Play

The player to the left of the dealer goes first.

When it's your turn, you can take a face-up card from the table with a matching card in your hand. That's called *taking a trick.* You put the cards from the trick in a face-up pile, called *a bundle,* in front of you. If you don't have a card that matches one on the table, you put a card from your hand face up with the others on the table. Then the player on your left tries to take a trick, and so on around the table. Each time someone takes a trick, he puts the two cards face up on top of his bundle.

Here's the exciting part. Instead of taking a trick on your turn, you can steal any player's bundle *if* you have a card in your hand that matches the top one on that bundle. Of course, someone may swipe your bundle on his next turn!

50

Whoever has the most cards in his bundle when the stock is gone is the winner.

P.S. Cards match when they have the same number or picture on them, not the same suit.

SUIT OF ARMOR

This is a very easy game to learn and play. You want to be the first player to have all the cards in your hand belong to the same suit—clubs, hearts, spades, or diamonds.

Dealing

Shuffle and cut the cards. Deal one card at a time to each player until everyone has seven cards. Put the rest of the cards in the center of the table.

How to Play

Look at your hand! See which suit you have the most of. If you have three clubs, a heart, two spades, and a diamond, for example, you'll want to try collecting clubs. But don't tell anyone which suit you're trying to collect!

The dealer starts. He puts one card of a suit that he doesn't want face down. Then the player on his left puts down a card he doesn't want, and picks up the card the dealer put down. Then the next player to the left puts down an unwanted card, and picks up the second player's discard. The play around the table goes on this way until one player has all seven cards of the same suit and cries, "Suit of Armor."

P.S. You may change the suit you want to collect as the game goes on.

BEGGAR-YOUR-NEIGHBOR

This is a fast, exciting game that depends strictly on luck. The point? To capture all the cards.

Dealing

Shuffle and cut the cards. Give each player twenty-six cards

How to Play

Hold your stack of cards face down in front of you. The person who didn't deal starts. He turns the top card of his stack face up, and puts it in the center of the table. The dealer does the same thing, putting his card on top of the first card. You both take turns turning over cards until one of you turns over an ace, King, Queen, or Jack. That's when the game really gets going.

Here's how. When player 1 turns over an ace or picture card, player 2 has to put extra cards from the top of his stack face up in the center pile as a penalty. He puts out four cards for an ace, three for a King, two for a Queen, and one for a Jack. If all the penalty cards are numbered 10 or under, the first player gets to take the whole center pile, including the penalty cards. He puts the pile face down underneath his stack of cards and puts out his top card to begin a new center pile. But if one of player 2's penalty cards is a picture card or an ace, everything is reversed. Then player 1 has to pay a penalty, and player 2 captures the cards.

Eventually one player will capture all the cards. This can take a short or long time. Whoever gets all the cards is the winner.

What makes this exciting is that you don't know who will win until the very last minute.

NIDDY NODDY

This is a very old game that children played in England 350 years ago. The point of the game is to be the first one out of cards.

Dealing

Shuffle and cut the cards. Deal out all the cards, one at a time. It doesn't matter if some kids have an extra card.

How to Play

The player to the left of the dealer starts. If she has a pair, she puts one of the two cards face up in the middle of the table, saying, "Here's a good card for thee." (*Thee* is an old-fashioned way of saying you.) If she doesn't have a pair, she passes, and the player on her left starts.

Once someone has put out a card, the next player to the left must put down face up a higher card of the same suit, saying, "Here's another as good as he." (In this game, ace is low.) If she can't put down a higher card, the player to her left has a turn, and so on.

Then the next person to the left puts down a still higher card of the same suit if he can, saying, "And here's the best of all three." If he doesn't have a higher card, he passes.

Play goes to the left again, and the next player must put down the fourth card, a still higher card of the same suit if she can, saying, "And here's old Niddy Noddy." If she can't, she passes. After the Niddy Noddy card is put down, the cards in the middle are turned face down. The player who put down the Niddy Noddy card starts a new round, playing one card from a pair she holds on top of the face-down card pile.

Suppose someone puts down a high card to start with? Once the King has been played, you have to turn the pile in the center over and start again. Whoever gets rid of her cards first, wins.

DONKEY

Here's a fun variation on the game of Pig. The point in this game is to avoid being the DONKEY by snatching one of the buttons in the center of the table when the time comes.

The more who play,
the sillier the game will be.

Dealing

You need one set of four matching cards (numbers or pictures) for each player. If six kids are playing, for example, you'll need six sets of four matching cards, or twenty-four cards. You'll also need some buttons. Put one *less* button than there are players in the center of the table. For six players, you'll need five buttons.

Shuffle the sets of cards together and cut. Deal one at a time to each player until they're all gone.

How to Play

When the dealer says, "Go!" pass a card face down to the person on your left and pick up the card passed to you from your right. Keep passing and picking up cards as quickly as possible, checking to see if you have four matching cards. Eventually someone will end up with four of a kind in her hand. Then she can grab a button; she must try to do it without anyone noticing. Everyone else grabs a button as soon as they notice her doing it.

One kid won't get a button. That player has the letter *D* (for donkey) marked down against her.

56

Shuffle, deal, and play again. If the same person doesn't get a button again, she now gets an *O* next to her *D.* Or perhaps someone else will get a *D* marked against her. The game is over when one player gets all six letters: *D-O-N-K-E-Y.* She is the donkey and must bray "Hee-haw!" as she runs around the other players.

P.S. Check after button grabbing to make sure that the winner *does* have four of a kind. If not, she's the donkey right away.

FOLLOW SUIT

Number of Players 4 to 6

Here's another game where the suit of the card, not its number, is important. But this game is a little complicated. The point is to take as many tricks as you can.

Dealing

Shuffle and cut the cards. In a game with four players, deal nine cards, one at a time, to each one. With five kids, deal eight cards to each. With six, deal seven. Put the rest of the cards face down on the table in a pile. That's called the *stock*. Turn the last card dealt to the dealer face up. The suit of that card is *trump*.

P.S. *Trump* means a suit that is super special. *Any* card of the trump suit is higher than cards of any other suit. Make sure you remember what the trump suit is!

How to Play

The player on the dealer's left starts. That person puts any card face up in the center of the table. The player to his left must put down another card of the same suit, and so on around the table. If you don't have a card of the right suit, you may play a trump or any other card. After each player puts down one card, the player who put down the highest card wins the pile of cards in the center. That's called *taking the trick.* Ace is the highest in this game, but *any trump card is higher than an ace of any suit.*

When you win a trick, put all the cards in your hand, then pick one to place face up in the center of the table. That leads (or starts) the next trick.

A player who is out of cards drops out.

The winner is the player who is still holding cards after everyone else has dropped out.

SPIT

In this game, you have to be alert as well as fast! The record time for a game between kids who were real experts was only two minutes.

This isn't a game to play with your little brother or sister. It's the most fun with someone who is just about as good as you are.

Dealing

Shuffle and cut the cards. Divide the deck into two equal piles. Each player gets one pile, called his *stock*.

How to Play

Hold your stock in one hand, face down. Both of you put four cards from your stock face up in front of you. That's called your *spread*. The whole idea is to be the first to use up your stock and spread.

Now you're ready to start. You play at the same time: Count together, one . . . two . . . three . . . SPIT. On the word SPIT you each slap the top card of your stock face up between the two spreads, starting two center piles. You get rid of your spread cards by putting them on top of your center pile or your opponent's center pile. BUT you can only put a card on a center pile if its rank is one above or one below the top card on the pile. If one pile has a 3 on it, you can put a 2 or 4 on top of the 3. If you put a 4 down, you can put a 3 or a 5 on that, and so on. Play your spread cards as quickly as possible.

When there's an empty place in your spread, fill it with a new card from your stock.

When neither of you has a spread card that you can put on a center pile, stop for a break, then say, One . . . two . . . three . . . SPIT again, slap the top card from your stack on your center pile, and keep going until one player has no more cards in his stock or spread. Whoever is out of cards takes the smaller center pile to be his new stock. The other player takes the larger one.

Shuffle your stock and start again. Keep playing until one of you is completely out of cards. That's the winner.

P.S. One important rule: You can only use *one hand* (the hand not holding your stock) to put cards on the center pile.

AUTHORS

This is a more complicated version of Go Fish. It's sometimes played with special card decks that show pictures of famous authors and their books. But you can play it with regular cards, too. You try to form *books* of four cards that show the same number or picture—four Kings, four 8s, four aces, and so forth. Count on your memory to help you win.

Dealing

Deal out the cards one at a time until they're all gone. It doesn't matter if some players get an extra card.

How to Play

Put all your matching cards together. Here's how your hand might look if four kids are playing:

The player on the dealer's left starts. When it's your turn, you ask another player for a card you need to complete a book. You have to name the player you're asking and the rank and suit of the card. And you can only ask for a card if you have at least one card with that number or picture in your hand.

Here's an example: Alexander, Gavin, Zoe, and Vanessa are playing. Alexander has the ace of spades and the ace of diamonds. He needs the two other aces to make a book, so he says, "Gavin, do you have the ace of hearts?" If Gavin has it, he must give it to Alexander, and then Alexander can ask Gavin or someone else for another card. But if Gavin doesn't have the ace, Alexander's turn is over. If Gavin has the ace of clubs, he doesn't have to give it to Alexander. The player on Alexander's left has the next turn.

> **Strategy hint:** Listen carefully when people ask for cards. Zoe has the turn after Alexander and she has the ace of clubs. Because she was listening she knows that Alexander has at least one ace and Gavin has none. She can figure out who has the ace of hearts. Can you?

Each time someone makes a book, he or she shows it to everyone and puts it face down on the table. When all the cards are gone, the winner is the player with the most books.

Number
of
Players
5 to 10

I DOUBT IT

This is a game in which it's okay to cheat. In fact you have to lie to play the game. You try to make everyone believe you are telling the truth about the cards you put down, even when you're not. (That's the only way you can get rid of your cards.)

Dealing

Use *two* decks of cards shuffled together. Deal two at a time until they are all gone. It doesn't matter if some players get an extra card or two.

How to Play

Sort the cards in your hand from lowest (ace) to highest (King).

The dealer starts. He must put one to four cards face down in the center of the table and announce how many and which cards they are. The catch is that players must follow this order in putting down cards: The dealer puts down aces, the next player 2s, the next 3s, the person after that 4s, and so on up to Kings. Then the next player starts with aces again.

So the dealer, for example, has to start out saying, "Two aces." If he doesn't have aces, he can cheat. He can *say* two aces even if he is putting down two 6s.

If a player suspects the dealer is lying, he can call out, "I doubt it," and turn over the dealer's cards. If they are aces, just as he said, the accuser has to pick up *all* the cards in the center and put them in his

64

hand. But if the dealer lied, *he* has to take the whole pile in *his* hand.

If everyone believes the dealer, the player to his left goes next. He is supposed to put down 2s.

After each player puts down his cards and announces what they are, any player can call out, "I doubt it." If you cheat and are discovered, you have to pick up the whole pile of cards in the center. But if a player accuses someone who didn't lie, that player must take the pile.

The winner is the first person to get rid of his or her cards. You won't be able to do it without cheating some of the time.

> **Strategy hint 1:** Play your hand quickly. People are more likely to doubt you if you spend a lot of time choosing the cards to put down.
>
> **Strategy hint 2:** Cheat early in the game. People are more likely to doubt you when you have only a few cards left.

TWENTY-NINE

You have to be good at addition to play this game well, so brush up on your math facts *before* you start! You want to be able to choose the right card to make the center pile of cards add up to exactly twenty-nine. Then you'll capture the cards.

Number of Players
4
You can play as partners, 2 against 2

Dealing

Shuffle and cut the cards. Deal one at a time to each player until all the cards are gone. Each player should have thirteen cards.

How to Play

Arrange your cards by how many points they are worth.

- Ace, King, Queen, and Jack = 1 point each.
- Number cards are worth the amount shown on the card, for example, a 5 is worth 5 points.

Partners show each other their cards. Then they sit across from one another. (You don't have to play partners.) The player on the dealer's left starts. She puts any card in her hand face up in the center of the table. The player to her left puts another card on top, adds up the card total so far and announces it, then the next person does the same, and so on.

Your object is to be the one—or help your partner be the one—to

66

put down a card that makes the pile total 29 points. That person (or partnership) wins the cards in the pile, and puts out a card to start the next pile.

You can put down any card you want on your turn, but you *can't* put down a card that makes the total go *over* 29 points. If each of the cards in your hand would make it go over 29, you must pass.

Keep each pile you or your partner win separate. When everyone is out of cards, the player or partners with the most piles win.

If no one can put down a card without the total going over 29 points, the game ends. Whoever has the most piles is the winner.

Strategy hint 1: If you can't make 29 points on a turn, play the lowest card you can.

Strategy hint 2: Be a card detective. Watch carefully to see which cards the other players don't have. Suppose the pile adds up to 25 points and it is Ginny's turn. She puts down a Queen. You can figure out that she doesn't have a 4 because otherwise she'd play it to win the pile.

CRAZY EIGHTS

Card historians think Crazy Eights was invented over 200 years ago in England, and that it was first called *Comet* after the comet predicted by Edmund Halley. Now the game is sometimes called *Eights,* and sometimes *Crazy Jacks.* But the point of all of them is the same: to be the first player to get rid of all his cards with the help of a *wild* card.

Dealing

Shuffle and cut the cards. With two players, deal seven cards to each. With more players, deal five cards to each. Put the rest of the cards face down in a pile in the center of the table. This is called the *draw pile.*

Turn over the top card in the draw pile to start a pile of face-up cards next to it. This is the *discard pile.* If the turned over card is an 8, bury it in the middle of the draw pile and turn over another card.

How to Play

Start with the player on the dealer's left. Everyone takes turns putting a card from their hand face up on the discard pile. That sounds easy. But it has to match the number, picture, or suit of the top card on the pile, or it can be an 8. In Crazy Eights, any 8 is a wild card. That means you can change its suit to whatever you want it to be.

Here's an example of how the game works. If there is a 4 of hearts

on top of the discard pile you have to put down another 4 of any suit, any card with hearts on it, or any 8. If you put down a 4 of clubs, the next player has to put down another 4, any card with clubs, or an 8. If you put down an 8 you can change its suit to whatever you wish. Then the next player will have to put down another 8 or a card with the suit you've chosen.

If you don't have a card with the right number or suit or an 8, you keep drawing from the draw pile until you get one you can put down.

P.S If the draw pile is gone, you have no card you can put down, and the game hasn't ended, you have to pass.

The game ends when one player is out of cards; that player is the winner. It also ends if no one can play any more cards, and the draw pile is all gone. Then the player with the fewest cards wins.

The winner collects points from the cards left in everyone else's hands.

Here's how to score:

- Eights   50 points each
- Kings, Queens, Jacks   10 points each
- Aces   1 point each
- Number cards   The number of points is the same as the number on the card. A 4 equals 4 points.

Set up a goal. The first player to reach 200 points, for example, can be the winner.

Strategy hint: You can play an 8 whenever you want to, but it's best to use them only:
1. When you have to
2. When you have a lot of cards of one suit that you want to get rid of
3. When another player has only one or two cards left.

You want to make sure you don't have it in your hand when a player runs out of cards. If you do, he or she will get 50 points!

HEARTS

This game used to be called *Reverse*. Why? Because the point of the game is to get the *least* points by not winning any hearts. Watch out!

Dealing

Shuffle and cut the cards. Deal one at a time to each player until they are all gone. All players should have thirteen cards.

How to Play

Organize your hand so that all the cards of each suit—clubs, spades, hearts, diamonds—are in order from low to high. Two is low; ace is high.

Choose three cards from your hand that you don't want. Pass them face down to the player on your left. Then pick up the cards that have been passed to you and organize your hand again.

Strategy hint 1: Pass the ace, King, Queen, Jack, or 10 of hearts if you have them.

The person on the dealer's left starts. If that's you, put any one of your cards face up in the middle of the table. This is called the *lead card*.

The player on your left puts a card of the same suit on top of the lead card. Then the player on her left goes, and so on. Whoever plays the highest card in that round takes the trick. That means she takes all four cards and puts them in a stack in front of her.

The player who takes the first trick leads the next round by putting out any card she wishes.

If you don't have a card of the same suit as the lead card, you can put any card you wish on top of the stack. It can't win the trick no matter how high it is.

Strategy hint 2: You don't want to win tricks that contain hearts. So put out low cards when you have to lead. Save your high cards to play when you can see that there are no hearts in the trick. Play hearts when you don't have any cards with the suit of the lead card.

Keep leading and taking tricks until everyone is out of cards. Then you count the number of hearts in the tricks you've won. Each heart counts one point. The player with the least hearts is the winner.

That's the simple version of Hearts. Now try a variation.

BLACK LADY

Dealing and playing in Black Lady are the same as in Hearts except for one thing. You don't want to get the Queen of spades (the Black Lady) in a trick either. If you end up with it, the Queen of spades counts 13 points! And that's added to the hearts in the tricks you've taken.

> **Strategy hint:** When you pass your three cards, make sure you pass the ace and King of spades if you have them. Otherwise you might end up taking a trick that has the Queen of spades in it. If you have the Queen of spades, hang on to it. Put it down when someone plays the King or ace of spades or when you are out of the suit needed for a trick.

For something risky and exciting try *Shooting the Moon*. That's when you try to *win* all 13 hearts and the Queen of spades. If you make it, you win the game and 26 points are added to every other player's score.

FAN TAN

Number of Players 3 to 8

No one knows how this game got its name. Some people think it is named after a Chinese gambling game, Fan Tan, in which you guess the number of soy beans in a pot. But in this game the point is to be the first player to get rid of your cards. The only catch is that you have to get rid of them in a special way.

Dealing

First give each player the same number of chips or counters such as buttons. Everyone puts one into the center of the table. This is called the *pool*.

How to Play

The player to the left of the dealer goes first. The game starts when someone is able to put a card with the number 7 face up in the middle of the table. If the player to the left of the dealer can't, she puts one chip in the pool and passes. Then the player on her left takes a turn, either playing a 7 or passing, and so on around the table.

Once a 7 has been played, you have three choices when it is your turn: (1) you can play another 7; (2) you can play a 6 or 8 of the same suit as the first 7; (3) you can pass because you don't have any of those cards. Here's how it works:

Emily puts down a 7 of hearts. Christina, on her left, puts down an

74

8 of hearts above the 7. That's called *building up.* Nell, on her left, puts down a 7 of clubs next to the first 7. Matthew, on her left, puts down a 6 of clubs. (If he had a 6 or 9 of hearts or 8 of clubs or another 7, he could have played one of those.)

This is how their cards would look on the table.

You can't play any number in a suit until the seven has been played. In this game ace is lowest; King is highest.

On the next round Emily could play another 7, a 6 or 9 of hearts, or a 5 or 8 of clubs.

The whole point is to get rid of your cards by putting down a 7 or building up or down on the 7s already on the table. If you can't put anything down, you must pass and put a chip in the pool.

The player who gets rid of all her cards first is the winner. The other players must put one chip in the pool for each card they have left. The winner takes the whole pool.

Strategy hint: If you can play more than one card on your turn, play a card from the suit you have the most of. Guess why!

CASINO

Both kids and adults who tried out the games in this book found this was one of the most exciting ones. It's a good choice when you want to play cards with your parents. You may find yourself hooked on it, too! But pay attention to all the steps in the directions because Casino is complicated to explain, even though it's not that hard to play. In fact, kids can often beat grown-ups!

Dealing

Shuffle and cut the cards. Deal two cards at a time until each player has four. Put another four cards face up in the center of the table. Set aside the remaining pack of cards. When the players use up the four cards in their hands, deal another set of four to each and so on throughout the game. When the four face-up cards are gone, deal out four more throughout the game.

How to Play

The player on the dealer's left starts.

When it's your turn, you want to take a face-up card from the middle of the table by matching it with one in your hand if you can. That's called *taking a trick*. There are three ways you can do it:

1. You have a card in your hand that matches a face-up card. Put yours on top of the matching card and take

76

both as a trick. If you have a 5 and there is a 5 on the table, for example, you can take it. If there are two 5s on the table you can take both on one turn. (You can't take two picture cards—King, Queen, or Jack—on one turn.)

2. You have a card with a number that is equal to the numbers on two or more face-up cards added together. You can take all on one turn. For example: a four and a two are among the face-up cards. You have a 6 in your hand, so you can take both. Ace equals one. If three or four face-up cards add up to a number in your hand, you can take all of them in a trick.

3. You can *build* a trick on one turn and take it on the next. Suppose you have a 2 and 7 in your hand and there is a 5 among the face-up cards. On one turn you put the 2 on top of the 5 and announce, "Building 7." On your next turn you take the two cards with your 7.

P.S. You can only build a number you have in your hand. And you must take your build on your next turn.

But beware! There is a danger in building. Another player who also has a 7 may take the two cards before your next turn! Or someone who has a 9 may pick up the built-up 7 and a 2 on the table, because $2 + 2 + 5 = 9$. Or someone may build on top of your build. He could put an ace on top of the 5 and 2, announcing, "Building 8."

You won't always be able to take a trick or build. If you can't, you must put one of the cards in your hand face up with the others.

The game ends when all the cards have been dealt and no one has any cards left. The player who took the last trick gets any extra face-up cards on the table.

Now it's time to add up everyone's score. Check with this table to figure out how many points you have.

The player with	Points	
The MOST cards	gets	3
The MOST spades	gets	1
The Big Casino (10 of diamonds)	gets	2
The Little Casino (2 of spades)	gets	1
An ace (each ace counts 1 point)	gets	1

The player with the most points is the winner.

ROYAL CASINO

This game is played exactly the same as Casino is played except for one thing. In regular Casino you can't build on a King, Queen, or Jack. You can only take them with a matching card. But in Royal Casino each picture card has a number value: Jacks count 11 points; Queens 12 points; Kings 13 points; and aces can be either 1 or 14 points. If you have a King in your hand and a 5 and an 8 are on the table, you can take them. Or you can build 12 points by putting an ace on a Jack and then take the cards with a Queen from your hand.

BLACKJACK

This fast-moving game was invented in France, where it is called *Vingt-et-Un* (vant-ay-unh), which means twenty-one. There's one very unusual thing about this game—each person plays against the dealer. You win if you get Blackjack—cards that add up to 21 points—or if your cards add up to a number closer to 21 than the dealer's cards. But if you go over 21 points, you go *bust* and are out. This game is a little complicated to play, so plan on a few practice rounds before you really get going. Winning doesn't just depend on luck.

Dealing

Pick someone to be the first dealer. When someone gets Blackjack he becomes the next dealer.

P.S. The traditional way to pick a dealer in Blackjack is by giving a face-up card to each player until someone gets an ace.

Shuffle and cut the cards. Most people bet buttons or chips when they play this game, but you don't have to. If you do, give each player at least thirty chips or buttons. Put extra chips in the center of the table. That's called the *kitty*. You put all your bets down before you get any cards.

Give everyone one card face down. Then go around again, dealing each player a face-up card.

How to Play

Everyone looks at their cards and silently adds up their points to see if they have Blackjack—exactly 21 points. Picture cards are worth 10 points, aces can be 1 or 11, and number cards are worth the number shown on them. If the dealer has a Blackjack, he shows his cards. He wins and that hand is over. If you're playing for chips, he collects everyone's bet from them. Any other player with a Blackjack collects only the dealer's bet from him. If both the dealer and a player get Blackjack, the dealer and player split everyone else's bets.

However, if just one player or no players have Blackjack, the game isn't over. Then the dealer asks one player at a time, "Do you stick?" In Blackjack language that means: "Do you want to keep just the cards you have, or do you want another one to see if you can get your total card points closer to 21?" You can get as many more cards as you want.

Sometimes it's hard to decide if you want more cards because you don't want to risk getting more than 21 points and going bust. Check the strategy hint for help.

> **Strategy hint:** The basic rule is to ask for another card if you have 13 points or less. If you have 17 points or more you should stick. With 14, 15, and 16 points, check the dealer's face-up card before deciding. If it's an ace, picture card, or 10, play safe and stick.

A player who says, "Hit me," gets another face-up card from the dealer. He can keep saying "hit me," and getting cards until he says, "I stick," or goes bust. Anyone who goes bust says, "I fold." He turns his cards over, and gives the dealer his chips. A player's turn ends when he sticks or busts.

Then the dealer asks the next player to his left, "Do you stick?" and so on around the table. The dealer has the last turn.

Everyone who didn't go bust turns over their cards. If the dealer goes over 21, he pays everyone still in the game the amount he bet. If the dealer's cards are closest to 21, the other players pay him the amounts they bet. The dealer pays his bet to any player who is closer to 21 than he is.

Collect the cards and put them face up at the bottom of the deck. The dealer doesn't reshuffle until he reaches a face-up card.

RUMMY

There are lots of rummy games. This is the basic one. Once you've played it, you'll find all the variations easy to understand. Rummy is a good game to play with grown-ups because they usually don't get bored.

Dealing

Shuffle and cut the cards. Deal them face down, one at a time. The amount of cards each player gets depends on the number of kids playing. For two players, give ten cards each. For three or four, give seven, and for five or six, give six.

Put the rest of the cards in a pile, face down. That's called the *stock.* Turn over the top card to make a discard pile next to it.

How to Play

In this game you try to get rid of your cards by grouping them together in *melds* and then laying the melds face up. A *meld* is a set of three or four of a kind, like three 4s or four Kings, or a sequence—called a *run*—of three or more cards of the same suit, like the 7, 8, 9, and 10 of clubs. In this game, ace is only low, so you can have a sequence of: ace, 2, 3, 4, but *not* Queen, King, ace.

Take a minute to put your matching cards and runs together before you start.

The player on the left of the dealer starts. Turns go to the left.

83

Take the top card from the stock or discard pile. If you have any melds, lay them face up like this:

Then put a card you don't want in the discard pile. And then it's the next kid's turn.

If you can put all your cards down in melds on one turn, that's *going rummy*. Then the game is over and you are the winner.

As the game continues, you may draw a card that fits in a meld you've already put down or in one someone else has put down. You can add that card to the meld when it's your turn. For example, if you or another player have a run of 2, 3, and 4 of clubs, whoever has the 5 or ace of clubs can put them into that meld.

You keep taking turns around the table until someone is out of cards. That person wins.

How to Score

Everyone puts their remaining cards face up. The winner gets points for all the cards left in everyone else's hands. Here's what cards are worth:

- Aces   = 1 point each
- Picture cards   = 10 points each
- Number cards   = the number on the card

Add up the winner's points, then shuffle, cut, and deal again. The first person to get 100 points is the Grand Rummy Champion. But you don't have to play for points. You can make the first person to win five games the champion.

> **Strategy hint 1:** Keep your eye on the discard pile so you know whether you can get the cards you need for the melds you're trying to make. You might have to try for a different one. If you know which cards other kids pick up from the discard pile, you'll know which melds they're trying to get.
>
> **Strategy hint 2:** Discard higher cards (like picture cards) that aren't matched early in the game. That way, if you lose, you won't give away so many points.

QUEEN CITY RUMMY

This game is just like basic Rummy except for three things. Scoring is different, everyone gets seven cards no matter how many players there are, and you must put down all your cards in melds on one turn. That means you have to wait until you have two complete melds in your hand before laying them down. The suspense is that someone else may do it first. Whoever lays down the melds first calls out "Rummy." That's the winner. She gets points for every card laid down. The other players get no points at all.

GIN RUMMY

This is the best rummy game for two players. It's like basic Rummy—you're trying to lay down the same kind of melds—but there are some very important differences. A lot of kids think Gin Rummy is more exciting.

Dealing

Deal ten cards to each player. Put the rest of the cards face down in a pile (that's the *stock*) and turn over the top card to start a discard pile next to it. That card is called the *up card*.

How to Play

Just as in basic Rummy you're trying to get all the cards in your hand to be part of a meld of three or more of a kind or three or more of a sequence in the same suit. But in Gin Rummy you lay down your melds and any extra cards only when you're ready to end the game in a showdown!

The person who didn't deal starts. Suppose that's you. You may take the upcard if you choose. But if you don't want it because it doesn't fit with any of the cards in your hand, you have to let the dealer have a chance to take it. If neither you nor the dealer want it, you draw the top card from the stock. Then you discard a card from your hand that you don't want. Then it's the dealer's turn to draw and discard. You keep drawing and discarding until one player knocks or says, "Gin."

86

If you don't have any unmatched cards—called *deadwood*—in your hand, you can "Go Gin." On your turn, you draw a card, lay down all your melds, discard a card face down, and call out "Gin." You win. The other player has to lay down all his cards, arranged in melds, with the deadwood to the side. The winner gets 25 points for going Gin. He also gets all the points from the other player's deadwood.

Here's what cards are worth:

- Picture cards   = 10 points each
- Aces   = 1 point each
- Number cards = the number shown on the card

But you don't have to wait to lay down your melds until you have exactly two melds and no extra cards. That's why Gin Rummy is full of suspense.

You can ask the other player for a showdown by "knocking" when you have 10 points or less of deadwood in your hand.

Here's how to knock: On your turn you draw a card, lay down your melds, put your deadwood to one side, discard one card face down, and knock the table once. You're taking a big chance because you don't know what the other player has in his hand.

Your opponent has to lay out his melds and deadwood when you knock. But he has one big advantage—he can try to get rid of his deadwood on your (the knocker's) melds. That means he can put an extra Queen, for example, on your meld of three Queens, or put a 6 of spades on your sequence of 3, 4, and 5 of spades. That also means that he can reduce his points of deadwood.

How to Score

You both add up your points in deadwood. If the knocker has the smaller number of points, he subtracts his score from the other player's. His score is the difference between the two. But if the other player has a smaller number, he gets the difference *plus* a bonus of 25 points. Why? Because the knocker was the one who wanted the showdown and he lost.

The winner deals the next game.

Keep playing until someone has 100 points.

P.S. The other player can't try to get rid of his deadwood when someone has "gone Gin."

Strategy hint 1: Knocking is risky. You want your deadwood to be worth as few points as possible, so save a few low cards as you play. Discard picture cards early on unless you have a pair. If you can't get a third picture in five or six turns, discard both.

Strategy hint 2: Knock as soon as you can when your deadwood is low cards. Often the other player knocks before you can "go Gin."

Strategy hint 3: Keep your eye on the discard pile.

ALL ABOUT POKER

Poker was invented in the United States. Maybe you learned about it from movies. In Hollywood westerns, cowboys and outlaws play poker in saloons and sometimes have a shoot-out over a game. In gangster movies, the games go on in smoky gambling rooms where everyone has a fat cigar in his mouth. The truth is that poker can be exciting even if you're playing in the family room, the car, or your own hideout.

You may be surprised to learn that there are hundreds of different poker games, many with funny names like Lamebrains, Spit in the Ocean, Hurricane, and Butcher Boy. But first learn the simplest versions of poker—One Card Poker and Two Card Poker. Then learn one basic kind, Draw Poker, before you start looking for variations.

Here's what makes all poker games similar. You win chips or counters by having the card or combination of cards with the highest rank (see What Beats What, page 90)—or by making people *think* you have the highest hand. Poker is a great game for people who are good at bluffing and faking.

Poker Chips

Poker chips are the way you keep track of what people bet on each hand. At the end of a certain number of rounds (the people playing the game decide how many), the player with the most chips is the winner. You can buy standard poker chips in variety stores, game departments, sometimes in sports shops, and stationery stores. They usually come in three colors: white chips are equal to 1; red, equal to 5; and blue, equal to 10. They can stand for points, pennies, candies, or anything you wish.

You can play poker without real chips. Just collect a bunch of buttons, beans, small stones, pennies, or anything else you have handy.

What Beats What in Poker

Except in one and two card poker, you always bet on five cards. In games where you get seven cards, you choose the five best to bet on. The five cards are called your *hand.* Combinations of cards are listed here from lowest rank to highest rank. A higher ranking one beats a lower ranking one.

1. High card: The lowest hand has five unmatched cards. If no one has a higher combination, the player with the highest card among the players wins. Ace is the highest; 2 is the lowest.
2. One pair: One set of two matching cards and three unmatched cards in a hand. A hand with a pair of Queens would beat a hand with a pair of 6s. If two players had pairs of Queens, the hand with the highest other cards would win.
3. Two pair: Two sets of two matching cards and one unmatched card in a hand, like two Kings, two 5s, and

a 3. A hand with a pair of aces and a pair of 3s would beat a hand with a pair of Queens and a pair of 7s.

4. Three of a kind: Three cards that match and two unmatched cards. Three Kings would beat three 4s.

5. Straight: Five cards in numerical sequence that aren't of the same suit. Two examples: ace of hearts, King of spades, Queen of spades, Jack of clubs, 10 of diamonds or 10 of clubs, 9 of hearts, 8 of diamonds, 7 of spades, 6 of hearts. The straight with the highest card beats one with a lower card.

6. Flush: Five cards of the same suit that aren't in sequence. An example: King, 10, 8, 7, and 4 of clubs. The flush with the highest card wins.

7. Full House: Three matching cards and one pair, such as three 7s and a pair of Jacks. If two players have a full house, the hand with the highest three matching cards wins.

8. Four of a kind: Four matching cards, such as four Kings or four 8s, and one unmatched card. The Kings would beat the 8s.

9. Straight Flush: Five cards in sequence that have the same suit. An example 2, 3, 4, 5, and 6 of clubs. A straight flush with higher cards beats one with lower cards.

10. Royal Flush: ace, King, Queen, Jack, and 10, all of the same suit. All suits are equal. You only have one chance in 650,000 to get this hand!

P.S. Here are some funny names for card combinations:

A *Washington Monument* means three fives, because the monument is 555 feet high.

An *American Airlines* means a pair of red aces.

Calamity Jane means the Queen of spades.

91

How to Keep a Poker Face

Keeping a poker face means not letting the expression on your face tell other players how good or bad your hand is. Try not to look disappointed if your cards are low. Don't look pleased if your cards are high. Other players will be watching to see if you smile when you bet or after you draw new cards. Practice having *no* expression on your face. Look cool—almost like you're not interested in how good your hand is.

Of course if you make the other players *believe* you have a high hand when you don't, they may drop out and *you'll* get the pot. You might have two Jacks in your hand but look as pleased as if you had four aces. That's called *bluffing.* It doesn't always work. Sometimes another player will stay in the game anyway. He's "calling your bluff."

SIMPLE ONE-CARD POKER

Number
of
Players
2 to 20

This is the very simplest poker game you can play. It's fun if you're stuck baby-sitting your little cousin (even four-year-olds can learn it) or if you're squashed into an airplane seat and can't manage too many cards.

Hint: If you're playing on an airplane, put the chips you bet in a cup.

Dealing

Give each player the same number of chips. Shuffle and cut the cards. Deal one card face down to each player.

How to Play

Peek at your card. Ace is the highest. The player to the left of the dealer has the first chance to bet one chip or pass. (Put the chips you're betting in the center of the table. That's called the *pot.*) When it is your turn, you can *drop,* which means you have a low card and want to get out of the game. You can *call,* which means your card is pretty good and you bet as much as the player before you. Or you can *raise,* which means you put in one or two chips more than the player just before you bet. Keep taking turns betting until everyone either drops or calls. During the betting is the time for bluffing. Do you really have a high card, or are you just pretending you do?

Then get set for the *showdown.* Each player who hasn't dropped out turns his card over. The player with the highest card wins all the chips. If two people tie, they split the pot. If all players but one drop out, the player who is left wins the pot, no matter how high her card is.

The winner deals the next time.

P.S. A way to get players with low cards to stick in the game is to play high-low. That means the players with the highest card and the lowest card split the pot.

TWO CARD POKER

This game is played the same way One Card Poker is. Deal two cards, one at a time, face down to each player. The highest combinations anyone can have is two aces. Any pair beats a single ace. A higher ranking pair beats a lower ranking one. For example, a pair of 10s beats a pair of 3s, and a pair of Kings beats a pair of Jacks.

Take turns betting. As in One Card Poker you can *drop* and get out of the game, *call* and make a bet equal to the one just before yours, or *raise* and add one or two chips more than the last player bet. When everyone stops raising, it's time for the *showdown.* When everyone still in the game turns over their cards, the player with the highest pair (or highest card if no one has any pairs) takes the pot.

The winner deals the next hand.

FIVE-CARD DRAW POKER

This is one of the two basic kinds of poker. It's more complicated than One or Two Card Poker.

Number of Players 2 to 8 can play but the game is most fun with 4 to 7

How to Play

There are seven parts to playing this game.

1. *Choose a betting limit.* You need poker chips or other counters. Give everyone an equal number, at least thirty. Decide as a group the most chips that you can bet at any one time, usually one or two until you've played poker a lot.

2. *Ante (an-tee) up.* Ante means before. So this is a bet before each deal. Everyone tosses one chip in the center of the table. This is the *pot.*

3. *Deal.* Choose a dealer by giving one card to each player until someone gets a Jack. That player is the first dealer. The player to his left will be the dealer for the next hand, and so on to the left. Shuffle and cut the cards. Deal five cards face down, one at a time, to each player. Start with the player on the dealer's left.

4. *First betting round.* Look at your hand. Do you have any good cards? Check what you have against the list What Beats What (page 90) if you can't remember what different combinations are worth.

   The player on the dealer's left has the first chance to bet. That's called *opening.* He can put one chip in the pot to open or he can pass. The turn goes to the player on his left. If everyone passes, the dealer collects the cards and deals again.

Once someone opens the betting, you can do one of two things when it is your turn. First, you can *drop* by putting your cards face down on the table and saying, "I'm out" or "I fold." This means you are out of the game because you think your cards aren't very good. (But remember that you are going to get the chance to exchange one or more of your cards.) You lose the chips you already put in the pot.

Second, you can stay in the game two ways. (1) You can match (the official word is *call*) the bet before yours by putting in enough chips to make your bet equal to the last player's bet. Usually you say, "I'll stay in." (2) Or you can *raise* the last bet by making your bet at least one chip higher than that bet. Usually you say, "I'll raise you one." Then the player on your left can *drop, match* your bet, or *raise,* and so on around the circle until everyone stops raising and drops or calls. If all the players but one drop, the player still in the game gets the whole pot.

5. *The Draw.* If you're still in the game, you can throw out any number of the cards in your hand—even all five—and get new ones from the dealer. The discards go in a separate discard pile. But you don't have to get any new ones. You can "stand pat," keeping them all.

Strategy hint: Now is the time when you can improve your hand. It's also your chance to bluff by giving the other players a false idea of how good your cards are. The big bluff is not drawing any cards at all, no matter how bad your hand is. That will make the other players think you have a great hand.

---

6. *Second Betting Round.* Look at your cards. How good is your hand now? The player who opened the first round of betting gets to bet or pass first. When betting is opened, you drop, call, or raise on your turn just the way you did on the first round.

   When everyone stops raising or if everyone passes, it's time for the showdown.

7. *Showdown.* All players still in the game put their cards face up on the table. Whoever has the highest hand takes the pot. Sometimes all but one player drops out before the end of the game, especially if everyone thinks one player has a very high hand. So that player wins— even if he was just bluffing—and doesn't even have to show his hand.

PASS THE GARBAGE

This game is played just like Draw Poker, but without the draw. Deal seven cards face down to each player. After the first round of betting, everyone picks the three worst cards in their hand and passes them face down to the player on their left.

Now everyone looks at their new hand of seven cards, picks out the five best cards as their final hand, and discards two cards.

Then start the second round of betting. When everyone drops or calls, have the showdown.

ALL ABOUT SOLITAIRE

Solitaire games are card games that you can play by yourself. (Solitaire/solitary, get it?) These games are great when you're home sick (but not too sick), when your best friend can't come over and it's raining, or when you just feel like being alone and quiet.

All solitaire games are sort of like puzzles. You lay cards down in a special pattern called a *tableau* (pronounced tab-low). Each game has a different pattern. Sometimes the cards are all face up, sometimes they're a combination of face up and face down. Then you pick up the cards in a special way, matching numbers, pictures, or suits. In some solitaire games you pick up two cards that add up to a special number or put cards in the tableau in sequence.

In other games you lay down additional face-up cards called *foundation* cards. Usually these are aces or Kings. Then you build sequences of cards up or down from them, using the cards in the tableau and your hand.

Does all this sound hard and mysterious? When you get started on a game you'll see that it's not.

Now, about winning. Lots of solitaire games are hard to win, because winning depends on how the cards fall when you lay them out. You can cheat, of course, because the only person who is playing is you. But it's more fun to see how often luck is with you. You can win all but one of the games in this book at least half the time.

COVER UP

This is the very easiest solitaire game. It only takes three minutes to play and you can win most of the time.

Deal and Layout

Shuffle and cut the cards. Lay out two rows of five face-up cards so no cards are touching each other, like this:

The rest of the cards are your stock. Keep them face down.

How to Play

Do you see any pairs? Good. You're going to cover up each pair among the ten cards in the tableau with cards from your stock. In the tableau above, you would put one card face up on each 8 and one on each King. Use the top card from your stock each time.

Now look again. Did those new cards create another pair? Or two? Cover each card in the new pair with the top card from your stock. Check again for pairs and cover them.

Keep covering pairs until your stock is gone. You've won!

P.S. There is only one way you can lose: if there are no pairs to cover before you use up your stock. Play five games and see how often it happens.

UP AND DOWN

You can almost always win this game. It's so easy that some people call it *Lazy Boy*.

In this game, you're going to build on a foundation instead of laying out a tableau. You'll need lots of space, so clear off one end of a table. Just shuffle and cut the cards.

How to Play

Hold the pack of cards face down and deal off three cards in a batch. Put them face up in a stack so you see only the top card. Put the next deal of three cards on top of it. Keep doing this until the top card is any King or ace.

Put the ace or King on the table. That is a *foundation* card. You want to build a sequence of the same suit up from the ace to 7 (ace, 2, 3, 4, 5, 6, 7) and down from each King to 8 (King, Queen, Jack, 10, 9, 8).

Keep turning over three cards at a time. Each time the top card is a foundation card—a King or ace—put it by itself on the table.

You can also use the top card to help you build a sequence you've started. Suppose you have an ace of diamonds and King of clubs out as foundation cards. Your top card is the 2 of diamonds. Put it overlapping the top of the ace like this:

Check the card that's on top now. Can you use it? If it's a Queen of clubs you can put it on the bottom of the King.

After you use the top card of your face-up deal, you can use the card under it.

When you've dealt the whole pack, turn it over and start dealing by threes again. Keep building or putting out aces and Kings as foundation cards. But if you go through the whole pack once without being able to use one card the game is over.

CLOCK SOLITAIRE

This solitaire game is easy to play but hard to win. Good luck!

Deal and Layout

Shuffle and cut the cards. Deal the cards face down one at a time into thirteen piles until all the cards are gone. You'll have four cards in each pile.

Arrange twelve piles as though they were the numbers on a clock, like this:

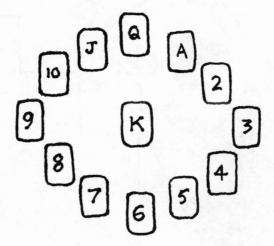

Put pile thirteen in the center of the circle.

How to Play

Each hour on the clock stands for a particular card. Ace is at 1 o'clock, 2 at 2 o'clock, 3 at 3 o'clock, and so on around the dial to

10 o'clock. Eleven o'clock is the Jack and 12 o'clock is the Queen. The center pile is the King.

Turn over the top card on the King pile.

Put that card under the correct pile for that number or picture. If it's a 9, stick it under the 9 o'clock pile like this:

Then turn up the top card in the 9 o'clock pile and stick it under the correct pile in the same way. Then turn up the top card of that pile and stick it under the right pile.

Do you get the idea? You want to get all the cards face up in their correct piles *before* all four Kings turn up. If that happens, the game is over and you have to start again.

P.S. You can also play for points. Give yourself 52 points if you succeed in getting all the cards face up before the Kings turn up. If you don't, give yourself 1 point for each face-up card. Play until you reach 100.

FOUR LEAF CLOVER

In this game you need to be able to add to fifteen to get rid of all the cards in the tableau and your hand. So brush up on all the ways you can make fifteen before you start!

Deal and Layout

Take the four 10s out of the deck and put them aside. You won't need them. Shuffle and cut the other cards.

Lay out a tableau of four rows of face-up cards with four in each row, like this:

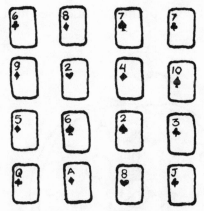

Keep the rest of the cards in a face-down pile. This is your stock.

How to Play

Look at the cards in the tableau. Do you see two or more cards of the same suit that add up to fifteen? Great! Aces count as 1 point. In the tableau above, the 7 of spades, 6 of spades, and 2 of spades add up to fifteen.

Take out the cards that add up to fifteen and put them to the side.

Fill the empty spaces in your tableau with cards from your stock, like this:

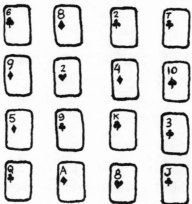

Look at the tableau again. Are there any cards now that add up to fifteen? In this tableau, you can make fifteen with the 9 and 6 of clubs or the 6, 7, and 2 of clubs. The best strategy is to use up as many cards as you can to make fifteen in one turn.

What about the Kings, Queens, and Jacks? They don't have a number value. You can only take them out of the tableau when all three—King, Queen, and Jack—of the same suit are showing. In this tableau, the King, Queen, and Jack of clubs can be removed. Fill any empty spaces with new cards from your stock.

Keep playing until all the cards in your tableau are gone. You've won!

But if you get stuck and can't find any cards in your tableau that add up to fifteen, the game is over. You can always try again.

PYRAMID

This is another solitaire game where you have to add—this time to thirteen. It takes some planning to win.

Deal and Layout

Shuffle and cut the cards. Lay out a tableau of twenty-eight face-up cards in seven rows. Start at the top with one card. Put two cards in the next row, overlapping the bottom of the first card. Then add a row of three cards, then four, then five, then six, then seven. You should have a pyramid of cards that looks like this:

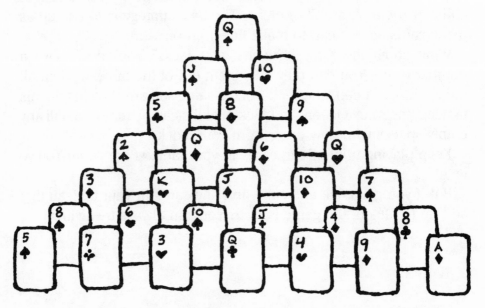

Keep the rest of the cards face down in a pile. That's your stock.

How to Play

The object is to try to take away all the cards in the pyramid. There are two catches. You can only take away cards when you have two that add up to thirteen. An ace counts 1, Jacks are 11, Queens are 12, and Kings are 13. You can take away a King by itself. It doesn't matter if the cards are the same suit. The second catch is that you can only take away cards that have no cards overlapping them at the bottom. That means you have to start with the cards in the bottom row of the pyramid.

But don't worry. You can use your stock to help you when you need to. (More on that in a minute.)

Look at the bottom row of your pyramid. Can you see any two cards that add up to thirteen? Put them in a discard pile. In the tableau above, the Queen and ace equal thirteen and the 4 and 9 equal thirteen, so they can be removed. Now some cards in the sixth row are uncovered, but they don't add up to thirteen.

It may be time for some help from your stock. Turn over the first card of your stock. If it can add up to thirteen with an uncovered card, put both in the discard pile. If not, turn over another card. Keep turning cards until you can make thirteen. As soon as you uncover a card in the tableau, you can combine it with another card to make thirteen.

When you have turned over all the cards in your stock, turn them face down and use them again.

Now we get to a third catch. You can only turn your stock over three times. You have to clear away the pyramid by then or the game is over.

P.S. Don't shuffle the stock when you turn it over.

107

SOLITAIRE

This is the game most people think of when they think of Solitaire games. Some people call it *Klondike,* others call it *Canfield,* and in England people call it *Demon Patience.* It's easy to play but hard to win. But be warned! Kids who tested this wanted to play it again and again and again and again.

Deal and Layout

Shuffle and cut the cards. Deal a row of seven cards, from left to right, with the first card face up and the rest face down. Then deal a row of six cards, overlapping the bottom of the face-down cards in the first row. Put the first card face up on the face-down card on the left. Put the rest of the cards face down. Then deal a row of five cards, with the first card face up on the column with two face-down cards on the left. Then deal a row of four, a row of three, and a row of two in a similar way. Finally, put one face-up card on the column of the face-down cards on the right. Your layout will have seven columns like this:

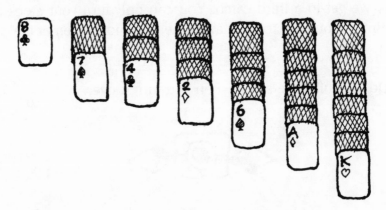

Keep the rest of your cards face down in a stack.

How to Play

This is more complicated than the other solitaire games because you have to build two different kinds of sequences at the same time. Follow the steps when you're learning to play.

Step 1. Is one of the face-up cards in your tableau an ace? If so, you're lucky! Put it aside and turn over the face-down card above it. You are going to build a sequence of cards of the same suit up from each ace. Look to see if there is a 2 in the same suit face up in the tableau. If so, put it on the ace. As you use face-up cards in building sequences, you can turn up the cards beneath them.

If you don't have any face-up aces or 2s, go to step 2.

Step 2. Look at the face-up cards on the tableau again. You're also trying to build sequences on the tableau. Some of the rules for the way you build them are different from building on the aces.

Rule 1: You have to build down in sequence. That means you can put a 5 on a 6, but *not* a King on a Queen.

Rule 2: You have to put a red suit on a black one, and a black one on a red one, like this:

Rule 3: You can move a sequence from one column to another to join sequences. The 3, 4, 5 can go on 6, 7, 8, 9 as long as the 5 is a different color than the 6.

Rule 4: When all the cards in a column are gone, you can

put a King in that space. Only a King can start a
new column.

Rule 5: You can only play cards that are face up. When you
move one, you can turn over the card it overlapped
and play that one.

Step 3. When you can't build any more sequences on the tableau,
turn over a set of three cards from your stock. If the top card can fit
in a sequence on the tableau, put it down. If it's an ace, put it aside.
After you've used the top card, use the card underneath.

Keep turning over sets of three cards until you find a card that can
fit onto a sequence you're building on the tableau, an ace to set
aside, or a card that can fit into the sequence you're building on an
ace.

Step 4. You're also trying to build sequences up on the aces you've
set aside. Here are the rules for building:

Rule 1: You must build *up* in sequence—ace, 2, 3, 4, and
so on up to King.

Rule 2: All cards in the sequence must match the suit of
the ace.

Rule 3: You can use only the face-up card in a tableau
column, or

Rule 4: When you turn over sets of three cards from your
stock you can use the top card.

If an ace shows up in your stock, put it out right away.

Step 5. You can keep going through your stock as long as you find
cards to put on any sequence. When you go through one time and
don't turn over a card you can use, *and* you can't use any more cards
on the tableau, the game is over. Better luck next time!

3
Make-Your-Own Card Games

HOW TO MAKE UP CARD GAMES

Does making up a card game sound hard? It's not. The games on the next few pages were made up by me and a lot of kids. They'll give you some ideas. Then make up your own.

You can use a regular card deck and just invent your own rules for dealing, playing, and winning. Remember that all card games were once invented by somebody! Or you can figure out a game to play with sports cards you already have, the way Zachary and Jackson did in their game Face, Back, or Mix Flip (page 114). Or you can design your own card deck the way Ashley and Fiona did for their Dotted Cinderella Game (page 124).

An easy way to invent a game is to model your own on one you already know how to play. Heads Up (page 122) is based on Concentration. Rhyming Fish (page 120) is based on Go Fish.

To make a card deck you need lots of three-by-five-inch index cards, scissors, felt tip markers, stickers, white glue such as Elmer's, and some old magazines.

If you want big cards, use the index cards as they are. For small ones, fold the cards in half and cut. When you make your deck of cards, you can follow the pattern of a regular card deck, but you don't have to. The main thing you need are sets of cards that match. The fifty-two cards in a regular deck, for example, are divided into thirteen different sets of four matching cards—4 Queens, 4 aces, and so on. Rebecca and Galen followed this pattern for their game, Slap It & Grab It (page 116). But you could make up a simple deck of twenty cards with just ten pairs. You can use pairs or sets of just about anything: flags, cars, favorite cartoon characters, shapes, flowers, colors (like Rainbow Flush, page 119), people (like Heads Up, page 122), animals (like Animal Snap, page 118), and so on.

Plan what kind of deck you want to make, then write, draw, or glue a picture on each card.

Play your game a few times to make sure that it works. You may have to change the rules a little. Then teach it to someone else!

ZACHARY AND JACKSON'S FACE, BACK, OR MIX FLIP

This game for two kids is based on flipping coins. You play it with baseball or other sports cards. The main thing is to have cards with a person's face on one side and writing or a blank on the other. Both players start with the same number of cards.

The players stand opposite one another and choose one to be the first caller. They each toss one card in the air, but before they do, the first caller guesses how the cards are going to land. He makes two calls—one for himself and one for the bonus pile. There are three possible calls: face, back, or mix. *Face* means both cards land face up. *Back* means both land face down. *Mix* means one lands face up and one lands face down. After the calls, both players toss the top card in their stack in the air at the same time and let the cards fall to the ground.

How to Play

Here's how it works: Jackson calls "face" for himself and "mix" for the bonus pile. If both cards land face up he gets them. If one card lands face up and one lands face down, they go into the bonus pile. If both cards land face down, Zachary gets them. Whoever wins the cards can pick up any bonus cards left from a previous call.

Whoever wins the cards sets them aside. Take turns calling and play until you use up all the cards in your stacks.

The player who wins the most cards is the winner of the game.

114

P.S. 1. Hold your card face down when you toss it.

P.S. 2. If a tossed card touches a person or table, the toss doesn't count. You have to do it over.

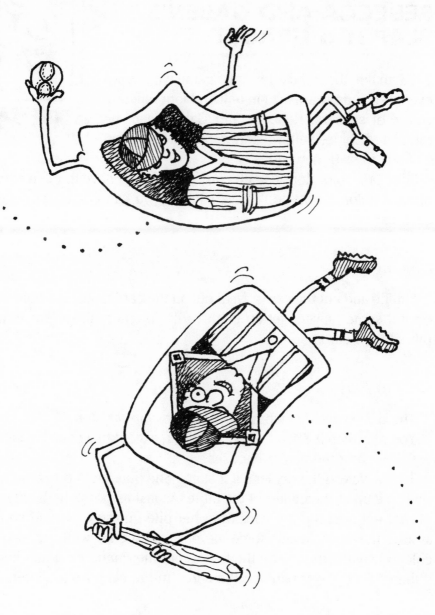

REBECCA AND GALEN'S SLAP IT & GRAB IT

To make the cards for this game you need twenty-six index cards cut in half and four different colors of stickers. Rebecca and Galen used the round red, blue, yellow, and green stickers you can buy in stationery stores.

Stick one color dot on each card. You should have thirteen cards of each color. If you don't have stickers you can color a circle on each card.

Dealing

Shuffle and cut the cards. Deal out all the cards, one at a time. It's okay if some players get an extra card. Players make a face-down pile of their cards.

How to Play

The dealer decides which color is the *slap it* color.

You play Slap It & Grab It like Slapjack, except that you slap cards with the color the dealer chooses.

The player on the dealer's left starts. She puts the top card in her pile face up in the center of the table. As fast as possible the player on her left puts the top card from her pile on top of it, and so on around the table. When someone puts out a card with the slap it color, everyone tries to be the first to put their hand on it and keep it there. That player wins all the cards in the center pile. She puts

116

them at the bottom of her face-down pile and tosses out a new card to start the next round.

When you're out of cards you're out of the game. The last player with cards is the winner.

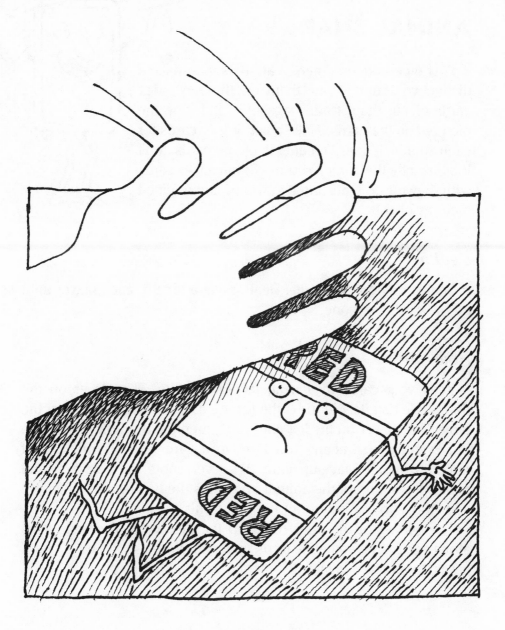

ANIMAL SNAP

First pick thirteen different animals that make a distinctive sound. Draw them on thirteen index cards or cut them from magazines and glue the pictures on the cards. Make a set of four cards for each animal. It doesn't matter if all four cards don't look exactly the same. You might have two cards with drawings of cats and two with different glued pictures of cats.

Dealing

Shuffle and cut the cards. Deal one at a time to each player until all the cards are gone.

How to Play

Keep your cards in a neat, face-down pile. The player on the dealer's left starts. He turns the top card of his pile face up on the table. The player on his left goes next, then the third player, and so on. Eventually someone will turn up a card with an animal that matches another face-up card. Whoever spots the pair first and makes the sound of the animal on it wins the two face-up piles. He adds those to the bottom of the pile in his hand.

The winner of the piles turns up the next card. Everyone goes along again until someone turns up a pair. When someone is out of cards, he is out. Play until someone wins all the cards.

RAINBOW FLUSH

Color a set of seven index cards seven different colors, like this:

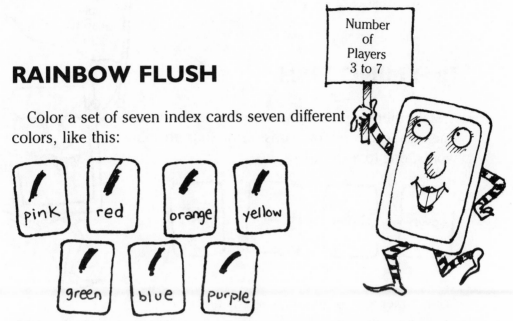

Make one set for each person playing. Three to seven kids can play.

Dealing

Shuffle and cut the cards. Deal seven to each player.

How to Play

Hold your cards in a fan. You're trying to be the first to gather all the colors of the rainbow in your hand.

When the dealer says, "Pass the rainbow," everyone puts a card with a color they don't want face down to their left. They pick up on the right the card passed to them. When the dealer says, "Pass the rainbow" again, they pass another card they don't want. Everyone keeps passing and picking up cards until someone has all seven different colors in her hand and shouts, "Rainbow Flush!" That's the winner.

119

RHYMING FISH

Make thirteen piles with four index cards in each one. On each set of cards print four rhyming words, one to a card, like this:

town   down   frown   gown

Some other sets of rhyming words are:

> hat, bat, mat, rat
> sock, lock, knock, rock
> hen, ten, pen, wren
> sun, fun, run, bun
> track, back, tack, sack
> lace, face, place, trace
> cane, rain, pain, main
> book, crook, look, cook
> bit, fit, mitt, hit

You think of the rest.

Dealing

Shuffle and cut the cards. Deal five to each player. Put the rest face down in a pile in the center of the table.

120

How to Play

Arrange your hand so that rhyming words are together. If you have any sets of four rhyming words, set them aside. You want to get as many sets as you can.

Whoever goes first asks any player for a card he needs to make a set. If Andy has crook and book, for example, he asks another player, "Give me a word that rhymes with crook." If that player has a rhyming card, he must give it to Jason. If he has more than one, he must hand over all of them. If he doesn't have any, he says, "Go fish for a rhyme." Andy draws a card from the center pile. If he gets a word that rhymes with crook, he gets another turn. If not, the turn goes to the left.

The player who has the most sets of rhyming words when the cards are gone wins the game.

HEADS UP

Number
of
Players
2 to 6

There are two ways to make a deck for this game: (1) Create a deck with twenty-six pairs of famous people—like two cards with pictures of President George Bush's head, two with Steffi Graf, two with Michael Jackson, and so on. You'll need two index cards for each person you choose. The two pictures don't have to match exactly. Print the name of the person on each card; (2) Or you can make thirteen sets of four famous people. Here are some categories you could choose:

4 American presidents   4 characters from books
4 basketball players   4 artists
4 rock stars   4 inventors
4 scientists   4 astronauts

Draw pictures or glue pictures you've cut from magazines on index cards. You'll need four cards for each set. Print the name of the person and the category on each card.

Whichever way you make your deck, the game is the same.

Dealing

Shuffle and cut the cards. Place them face down in four rows, like this:

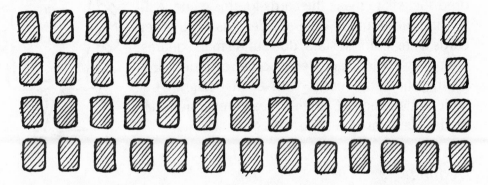

How to Play

You play Heads Up just the way you play Concentration.

The first player turns over two cards and says, "Heads Up!" If they make a pair, she keeps them and takes another turn.

If the cards picked up don't make a pair, the player shows them to everyone, then puts them face down in the same spot. Then the next player goes. Everyone tries to remember which cards they have seen so they can pick up a match. When all the cards have been paired, the game is over.

The player with the most pairs wins.

P.S. If you've made pairs of cards, it's easy to tell if the cards are a pair. If you've made sets of four, you must pick up two cards that belong to one set, like two presidents or two scientists.

ASHLEY AND FIONA'S DOTTED CINDERELLA GAME

Number
of
Players
3 or more

You need fifty-two index cards and lots of colored stickers to make the cards for this game. Ashley and Fiona made different designs on thirteen cards using colored stars, dots, and small squares. Then they copied each design on three more cards so they had four cards with each design. They added one special *Cinderella* card on which they made a very fancy design with gold stars.

Dealing

Shuffle and cut the cards. Deal out all the cards, one at a time. It doesn't matter if some kids have an extra card.

How to Play

Check to see if you have any matching designs. Put these pairs face down in front of you. Arrange the rest of your cards in a fan.

This game is the reverse of Old Maid. You want to end up with the Cinderella card.

The dealer starts. When it's your turn, pull a card from the hand of the player on your left. If you get a card that matches one in your hand, show the pair and put it with your other pairs. If it doesn't, just keep it in your hand. Turns go to the left.

When all the cards are paired, one player will be left with the Cinderella card. That's the winner.

4
The Best Card Tricks and Stunts

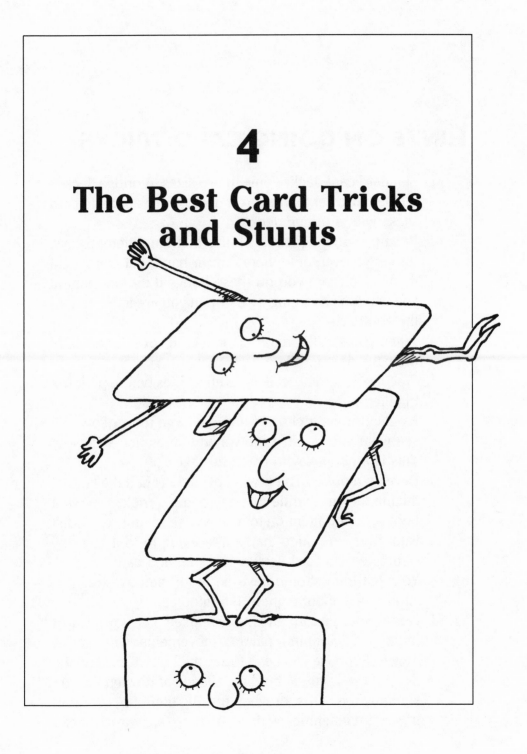

HINTS ON DOING CARD TRICKS

1. Standard card decks come in two sizes. A bridge deck is a little narrower than a poker deck. It's easier to do card tricks with a bridge deck.
2. Practice handling cards. Shuffle them in different ways, turn them over, hold them in your hand, cut them, deal them. The more you do these things the more natural you will look handling cards when you are trying to fool the audience.
3. When you shuffle in a trick, keep the cards as close to the table as possible.
4. Practice your tricks at least twenty times before performing them.
5. Practice doing tricks in front of a large mirror so you'll see what you do, just the way the audience sees you. This is a good way to catch mistakes.
6. Develop a *patter*. That's what magicians call the kind of talking they use while they are doing a trick. You want people to pay attention to what you're saying. You don't want them to notice that you're trying to fool them by turning over a card deck or peeking at a card.
7. Your program should have no more than five tricks. It should last about eight to ten minutes.
8. During your performance, stay relaxed. Go slowly. Most important, combine natural movements with secret moves. Suppose you need to see the bottom card on the deck of cards you're holding. Glance at it when you are shuffling the cards, or when picking them up, or squaring or straightening the deck. All these are ways you can

casually look at the bottom card without the audience getting suspicious. The more natural you can make it look, the more the audience will be fooled.

The first few times you try to look natural you will probably end up looking awkward. But just keep practicing.

9. While you're performing, you'll want to add suspense. Pause. Concentrate by putting your hand on your head and closing your eyes. Mumble magic words or rhymes you've made up. Pretend to be puzzled and then say, "Aha!"

ON THE EDGE CARD STUNT

Here's a quick and easy stunt to get your card act started. Ask for several volunteers from the audience. Challenge them to balance a card on its edge in five seconds. They won't be able to.

But you will! Hold the card in the palm of your hand, curving it slightly. Set it down on the table while it is still curved. It will remain curved long enough for you to balance it!

THE DIME-IN-THE-GLASS CARD STUNT

You'll need a heavy glass (not plastic) that is not too wide, a dime, and one card for this stunt. Place the card on top of the glass with the dime in the middle, like this:

Challenge a volunteer to get the dime into the glass without picking up or holding the card or knocking over the glass.

When they can't do it, show them how.

Flick your finger against the edge of the card. It will fly off and the coin will drop into the glass.

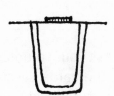

FIND THE CARD

You can learn how to do this simple trick in a few minutes. All it takes is a secret glance at the bottom card of the deck for you to identify any card your audience picks from the whole deck.

Here's what to do:

1. Ask for a volunteer from the audience to shuffle the cards so no one will think you've fixed the deck in a special way.
2. Fan out the cards and hold them so they face the volunteer. Ask him to pick any card, remove it from the deck, memorize it, and show it to the rest of the audience; he must not let you see it.
3. While he is doing this, you slide the cards into a pile, tapping the edges of the cards against the table to straighten them. Slyly sneak a look at the bottom card. Remember the number or picture and suit.

Hint: Practice glancing at the bottom card so you don't do it in an obvious way.

---

4. Put the deck face down on the table. Ask your volunteer to put his card on top and then cut the cards several times. That way he'll think his card is completely hidden in the deck.
5. Announce that you will now identify the card. Here's the

secret. When your volunteer cut the cards, the bottom card ended up on top of his card. The bottom card you memorized will be right on top of that card.

6. Start turning over the cards one at a time. Use your magician's patter and add suspense. Tap the top card of the deck and tell the audience you're using your magic touch to identify the correct card. Go very slowly.

7. When you turn over the card that you memorized, stop and tap the next face-down card. "Aha!" you can announce, "This will be your card. I feel the magic vibrations."

That will be the card your volunteer picked.

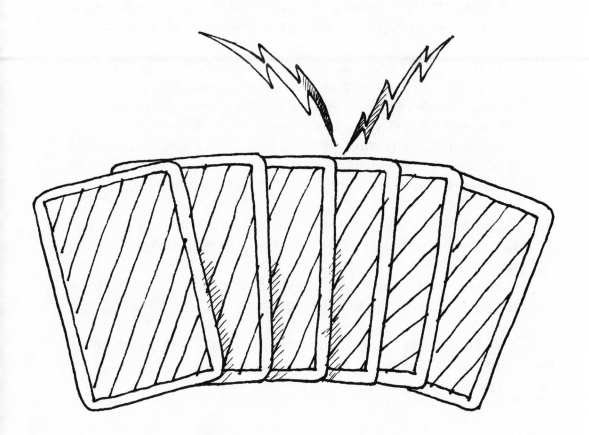

THE X-RAY EYE TRICK

Be warned. Your audience may ask you to do this trick again and again as they try to figure out your secret.

First, ask a volunteer to count out three piles of cards in a special way while your back is turned. He must follow the directions exactly or the trick won't work.

He holds the deck in one hand and turns the first card face up on the table. He starts counting with the number on that card, putting face-up cards on top of it until he reaches the number thirteen.

Here's how: If the card is an 8, he'll count the card he puts face up on top of it as 9, the card after that 10, then the one after that 11, then 12, then 13. After the volunteer reaches 13, he turns the cards in that pile face down and starts a new one.

In this trick ace is one, Jack is 11, Queen is 12, and King is 13. So if he turns up a Queen as the first card in a pile, he'll count that as 12 and put down only one face-up card on top of it to reach 13.

The volunteer counts out three piles of cards, turning each one face down as he finishes it. He puts the remaining cards in a pile to the side.

You turn around, count the number of cards in the pile of remaining cards, then ask the volunteer to turn face up the top card on any two piles.

You're going to use your X-ray vision to identify the top card on the third pile.

Concentrate hard.

To get the answer you have to do some secret arithmetic in your head. First you need the number of leftover cards. In this case it's thirty-one. Then you need to add the two face-up cards together. Here the cards are Jack and 5, so the sum is sixteen. Then add 10 to the sum (you always add 10, no matter what the face-up cards are). That makes twenty-six. Now you subtract that number from the number of leftover cards. So in this example, you'd subtract twenty-six from thirty-one. The answer you get will be the number of the top card in the third pile. Here, it's a 5.

Your answer will always be right!

P.S. Make sure your deck has fifty-two cards. If it doesn't, the trick won't work.

THREE-COLUMN CARD MAGIC

This foolproof trick depends on the way you pick up the cards. If you do it right, you'll have no problem finding any card chosen by someone in your audience:

How It Works

1. Ask for a volunteer from the audience to shuffle the cards. Then deal a row of three face-up cards, going from left to right. Next deal an overlapping row below it, then another, and another, until there are seven face-up cards in each column, like this:

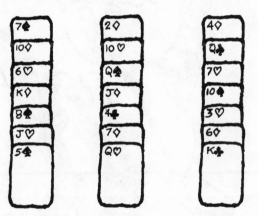

2. Ask the volunteer to visually pick a card and tell you which column it is in. Remind her not to tell you which card it is, to stare at it, or give you any other clues.
3. Slide the cards in each column together to make a pile. Don't change the order of the cards in each column.

4. For the trick to work, you must pick up the three piles in a special order. Put the pile that has the volunteer's card in it *between* the other piles.

5. Turn the cards face down and deal three columns again, just as you did before. Then ask your volunteer which column her card is in this time. (It's usually, but not always, in a different column.)

6. Pick up the cards again, making sure you keep the order of the cards in each column and that you put the column with the volunteer's card between the other two.

7. Deal again, just as before, and have the volunteer point to the column in which her card appears now. Pick up the cards in the correct order again.

8. Turn the cards face down. Use a little magician's patter. Say a few magic words over the cards or wave a magic wand over the card pile.

9. Turn over the cards slowly, one at a time, counting silently. Pause after you've turned over the tenth card. Close your eyes, then predict that the next card will be the chosen card.

The eleventh card will *always* be the volunteer's card.

THE SECRET DEAL

In this trick you're going to identify two cards chosen by someone in the audience. And you'll be able to do it just by the way you deal the cards.

Follow each step exactly:

1. Give the deck of cards to someone in the audience. Ask him to shuffle them and deal six face-down piles of five cards each.
2. Now ask him to choose and memorize two cards from the remaining deck without letting you see them. He can show them to the audience, but not to you.
3. Have him put the two cards face down on any two of the six piles. Make sure you notice and remember which piles he puts the cards on, but don't let anyone know that it is important to you.
4. You have to pick up the piles in a special order for the trick to work. Casually pick up one of the piles with an extra card first. Then slide two regular piles on top of it. Now put the other pile with the extra card on top, and then put the last two regular piles on top of that.
5. Deal all the cards into two piles, starting with one card on the left, then one on the right, then one on the left again, one on the right, and so on.
6. When all the cards are in two piles, ask your volunteer to choose one of the two piles. You'll adjust what you say according to which one he picks, because you need

to deal from the pile on your left. So if he points to the pile on the left, say, "We'll use the left pile for the rest of the trick." But if he picks the pile on the right, announce, "You'll have the right pile and I'll take the left one."

7. Deal the left pile into two piles, starting with one card on the left, one on the right, another on the left, another on the right, and so on.

8. When you're finished, pick up the new pile on the left and start dealing another two piles, one to the left and one to the right again, just as you did before.

9. Once again, pick up the pile on the left. It should have four cards in it. Deal two piles again, starting with the left, then the right, then the left, then right.

10. Pick up the pile on the left, turn over the cards, and announce, "These are your cards." They will be.

PILE
TO THE LEFT

NEEDLE IN THE HAYSTACK

This trick takes careful preparation and some good magician's patter so your audience won't catch on to the secret. Once again you're going to identify a card chosen by someone in the audience.

Here's how it goes:

Step 1. Before your performance, fix the deck so that all the red suit cards are in one pile and all the black ones are in the other.

Step 2. At the performance, hold one of the two piles face down in a fan, like this:

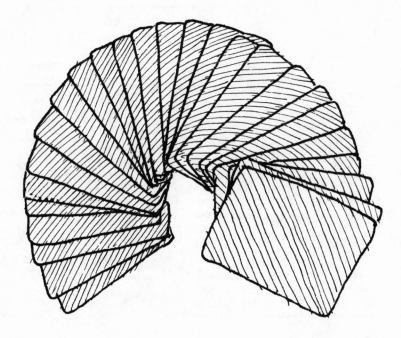

Put the other pile face down on the table where you can reach it easily. Ask for a volunteer from the audience to pick a card from the fanned cards you are holding.

Step 3. Tell her to write down what the card is without showing it to you or telling you what it is.

Step 4. Now for the tricky part. While she is concentrating on writing, you casually switch the two piles of cards, putting down the one you are holding and picking up the other pile.

Step 5. Then turn your back to your volunteer and hold that pile of cards behind your back. Ask her to put her card back into the pile that you are holding. Point out that you can't see the card she has picked.

Step 6. Turn around again and shuffle the pile of cards you're holding, keeping them close to the table. Look through the cards without letting anyone see them and pick out the volunteer's card.

Can you guess how you'll do it? If the pack has red suit cards, her card will be the black one. If the pack has black cards, her card will be the red one.

P.S. Hold the pile carefully so your volunteer can't see that all the cards are red or black.

THE AMAZING BLINDFOLDED CARD READER

Here's another easy trick to master. It will be very mysterious to your audience how you can tell which card a volunteer picked. Why? Because you'll be blindfolded. They key to the trick is to be able to add and subtract.

You'll need a pencil and paper as well as a blindfold and a deck of cards.

Step 1. Remove the ace, 2, 3, 4, 5, 6, 7, 8, and 9 of spades from your deck. Ask a volunteer to blindfold you. Then hand her the nine spades, the paper and the pencil.

Step 2. Ask the volunteer to pick any five cards (out of the nine cards) and add up their value. An ace counts as a 1. She should discard the other four cards.

Here's a sample:

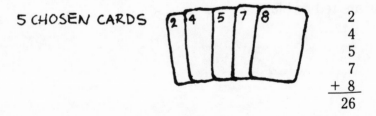

```
5 CHOSEN CARDS                          2
                                        4
                                        5
                                        7
                                      + 8
                                       26
```

Step 3. Have the volunteer pick one of the five cards. She can hide it in a pocket or give it to a friend to hold.

Step 4. Now ask your volunteer to put the four cards that are left in a row like this:

4
REMAINING
CARDS

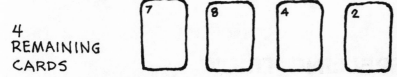

She must write down the four-digit number they make. (7842)

Step 5. Have your volunteer subtract the number she wrote down in Step 2 from the number she wrote down in Step 4 and tell you her answer. $(7842 - 26 = 7816)$

Step 6. Now it's time to identify the hidden card. Use some magician's patter while you're doing the arithmetic that will help you figure out what the hidden card is.

  You add all the digits in her answer together. The sample answer here is 7816. You would first add

$$
\begin{array}{r}
7 \\
8 \\
1 \\
+\ 6 \\
\hline
22
\end{array}
$$

and get 22.

Step 7. Then you add the two digits in that answer together. In this sample, you would add $2 + 2$ and get 4.

Step 8. Last, you subtract that answer from nine. For example, you would subtract four from nine. Your answer is the number of the hidden card! In this case it's five.

P.S. 1. If you get nine as an answer in Step 7, that is the number of the hidden card.

P.S. 2. Build suspense in this trick by tapping your forehead, muttering magic words or phrases, and wiggling your fingers in the air to catch the *vibrations* from the card.

THE SPELLING TRICK

This is a good show-off trick that little kids love to watch and that even six-year-olds can do. You're going to turn up the cards whose name or number you spell. It just takes a little preparation.

Here's what you do:

1. Remove the ace, 2, 3, 4, 5, 6, 7, 8, 9, 10, Jack, Queen, and King of one suit from your deck.
2. Arrange those cards face up in this exact order: 3 first, 8 (on top of the three), 7 (on top of the 8), Ace, Queen, 6, 4, 2, Jack, King, 10, 9, then 5.
3. Turn over the pile of cards. Now they are all face down.
4. Tell your audience that you will turn over the card whose name you spell, starting with the ace.
5. Holding the cards in one hand, put the top card at the bottom of the pack, and say, "*A.*" Do the same for the next card, saying the letter, "*C.*" Say, "*E*" as you put the third card at the bottom of the pack. Then say, "Here comes the Ace," and turn the fourth card face up. Put the ace on the table and continue.
6. Spell the next card, *T-W-O*, in the same way, by putting one card on the bottom of the pack each time you say a letter. Then turn over the fourth card, and put it face up on the ace. Say, "Here comes the two." Leave the 2 on top of the ace and continue.
7. Do the same thing for 3, 4, 5, 6, 7, 8, 9, 10, Jack, and Queen. Even when you only have a few cards, you put the top card at the bottom of the cards each time you say a letter. The last card will be the King.

THE INCREDIBLE FREE-FORM CARD TOWER

Do you have patience and determination? You'll need both plus a lot of practice to build this tower of cards.

Hint 1: Work with a friend. That way you won't get so frustrated. When the cards fall down for the tenth time, just laugh.

Hint 2: Build your tower on a flat rug, not a completely smooth surface. If you want to build on a table, spread out a tablecloth or placemat or even a sheet of paper toweling and built on top of that.

This is the way Jackson built his. It was the design that worked the very best.

What to Do

Hold the long edges of each card between your thumb and first, middle, and ring fingertips, like this:

143

Lean the top short edges of two cards against one another to make a tent, like this:

Lean cards against the two open ends, like this:

Then lean cards around the sides. This will make the bottom of your tower very stable. Make two more tents the same way, right next to the first tent. Your base should look like this:

Now make a floor. Hold a card so it faces the table and drop it *gently* on top of the tower base. Drop several cards so that they overlap until you have a solid floor, like this:

Build tents on top of the floor the way you built the base. Go slowly. Don't scream if the tower falls over!

Keep building floors and tents on top of them. Make your tower as high as you can. Believe it or not, some nine-year-olds built a tower with five levels.

Hint 3: A used, worn deck of cards works best.

CARD GLOSSARY

black card   A card with clubs or spades. In some solitaire games you put any black card on any red card.

cut   To lift off the top part of a face-down deck. Put the top on the table, and then put the bottom part of the deck on top. The player on the dealer's left cuts the cards after they have been shuffled.

deal   Handing out cards to the players from the deck. You deal the top card first, usually to the person on the dealer's left.

dealer   The person who shuffles the cards and hands them out.

deck   A regular set of fifty-two cards.

deuce   A card with the number 2 on it.

discard   To put down a card you don't want at the end of your turn. Usually you put it in a discard pile, right next to the rest of the deck.

draw   To take the top card from the rest of the deck after the cards have been dealt.

face card   A King, Queen, or Jack.

face down   This means the picture or number side of the card does not show.

face up   This means you can see the picture or number side of the card.

fan   To hold your cards so you can see the corner of each one, like this:

four of a kind   Four cards that match in number or picture but not suit, like four Queens, or four 10s.

follow suit   To put down a card of the same suit as the card just played.

146

foundation card A card you build up or down on in solitaire games. This card is usually an ace or King.

hand The cards you are holding in your hand during a game.

lead To play the first card. Usually the player to the left of the dealer leads.

meld A set of three or more cards with the same number or picture, or a sequence of three or more cards of the same suit, which is placed face up on the table. In all Rummy games this is how you win.

pack A deck.

pair Any two cards that match by number or picture, like two 3s or two Kings.

picture card A King, Queen, or Jack.

red card A card with hearts or diamonds on it. In some solitaire games you can put any red card on a black card.

round This means each person in the game has had a turn to play a card.

shuffle To mix up the cards so that the same suits and numbers aren't together. You always shuffle the cards before you start a game.

spot card Any card with a number on it or an ace.

spot value The value of the number on the card. The spot value of a 3 is 3 points.

stock The cards that are left over after dealing.

suit One of four special designs that appear on the cards. They are hearts, spades, clubs, and diamonds.

tableau The pattern in which you lay out cards in solitaire.

trick When each player puts one face-up card in the center of the table on one round of play, the pile of cards is called a *trick*. The highest card played wins the trick. In some games, such as Casino, you take a trick when you can match a face-up card on the table with one from your hand.

trump A number or suit you've picked to be extra powerful in a game, such as Hearts. Those cards will then be higher in value than any other cards.

wild card A card that can be whatever number or suit you want it to be. In the card game Crazy Eights, 8s are wild. In most games, jokers are wild.

INDEX